About the Author

Cristovam Buarque is a well-known Brazilian economist who from 1985 to 1989 held the office of Rector of the University of Brasília for a four-year term. Before that, he had been an advisor to former President Tancredo Neves and a member of the Special Commission entrusted with the task of drawing up the new Brazilian constitution. Among other public duties, he coordinated a study (published under the title, *Crime e Castigo da Dívida Externa*) at the request of the Chamber of Deputies' Parliamentary Investigation Commission on the problem of the country's foreign debt. He is also President of the Board of the United Nations University for Peace in San Jose, Costa Rica.

Dr. Buarque first graduated as a mechanical engineer. In 1973 he was awarded a doctorate in Economics at the Sorbonne. From 1973 to 1979 he worked as an economist for the Inter-American Development Bank, serving in Ecuador, Honduras and Washington D.C. Since 1979 he has taught in the Economics Department at the University of Brasília where he is now Professor of Economics.

He is the author of several books in Portuguese and Spanish, including:

A Desordem do Progresso

Avaliaçao Econômica de Projetos

Tecnologia Apropriada: Una Política para la Banca de Desarrollo

O Colapso de Modernidade Brasileira e una proposia alternativa.

The End of Economics?

Ethics and the Disorder of Progress

Cristovam Buarque

Translated by
Mark Ridd

Zed Books Ltd.
London & New Jersey

To
Antonio Gonzalez de Leon
and
Chico Mendes

The End of Economics was first published in English by Zed Books Ltd., 57 Caledonian Road, London N1 9BU and 165 First Avenue, Atlantic Highlands, New Jersey 07716, USA in 1993. Based on the author's original book, *A Desordem do Progresso: O fim da era dos economistas e a construção do futuro* (Editora Paz e Terra, Rua do Triunfo 177, 01212 São Paulo, SP, Brazil, 1990).

Cover designed by Andrew Corbett
Typeset by Ray Davies
Printed and bound in the United Kingdom by
Biddles Ltd, Guildford & King's Lynn

A catalogue record for this book is available
from the British Library
US CIP is available from the Library of Congress

ISBN 1 85649 097 1 Hb
ISBN 1 85649 098 X Pb

Contents

Contents

Chapter 6. The Power of Technology

Chapter 7. The Value of Nature

Chapter 8. The Value of Culture

Chapter 9. Thinking in a Third-World World

Foreword

With the end of the Cold War (it is to be hoped, for a very considerable length of time), socially equitable, environmentally prudent and economically viable development and the North-South divide are bound to become the central preoccupations of the international system. At least, the results of the Rio '92 Conference, the so-called Earth Summit, and the recent restructuring of the UN Secretariat point in this direction.

The tasks ahead are difficult. 'Real socialism' has collapsed. But late peripheral capitalism has brought, at best, to the countries of the South a lopsided modernization benefiting only a minority (what may be called the North in the South) and at the expense of an excluded or marginalized majority, not to speak of the high ecological costs involved. Even in the North, the economic models relied on are increasingly showing their weaknesses: structural unemployment, a shrinking welfare state, and a generally dismal economic performance.

The continuous imitative reproduction of these kinds of model in the South is neither desirable nor possible if one bears in mind the question of ecological sustainability. To protect our planet from destructive climatic change, it is necessary to alter drastically the development styles in the North while at the same time inventing original solutions for the South based on innovative patterns of resource use and a search for a civilization of 'being' based on an equitable sharing of 'having'.

The situation is further complicated by the current phenomenon of a decoupling of the financial sphere from the real economy. As a result, huge resources are being diverted towards sterile speculation in the 'world casino' at the expense of the production of actual wealth and human well-being.

Last but not least, the disappearance of the Soviet Union as a superpower reduces the bargaining capacity of the South in its relations with the North. The time has not yet come when we can see a new brand of non-alignment with the countries of the South exploring to their benefit the rivalries between the three competing mega-blocs

(North America, Japan and Western Europe) and, at the same time, expanding South-South cooperation. For the time being, one can only expect instead a reinforcement of asymmetrical and irreversible links between the North and the South.

A further complication comes from the dismal state of mainstream development studies which dominates the thinking and practice of so many governments and international organizations. The spread of neo-liberal orthodoxy presents what amounts to a solution of a free market utopia (in the literal sense of this word, such a system of course does not exist anywhere on the planet) and the minimum State. Almost exclusive emphasis has been put on the economic dimension of development, which in turn is equated simply with growth and private profit and not with an overall social evaluation of economic efficiency.

Modernization based on accelerating 'creative destruction' of accumulated capital and natural resources, and the use, all over the world, of modern techniques have become a veritable gospel. The alternative of submitting scientific and technical progress to social assessment and public choice has been all but abandoned.

In other words, development economics has become an ahistorical and value-free discipline with the pretence of being a science because of its extensive use of mathematical language. And the economic calculus has invaded all realms of human life, impoverishing to an extraordinary degree our understanding of human behaviour.

Under such circumstances, the task of combining social, ecological and economic concerns subordinated to an ultimate ethical regulation requires a major theoretical effort and a restructuring of development studies, including economics, so as to give them a historical dimension and the capacity to embrace the whole complex field of what I would call eco-socio-economics (as distinct from a more narrowly conceived ecological economics). Only in this way can the development sciences recover their heuristic and pedagogical value. Of course, real solutions can only come from praxis, that is, from the ongoing concrete historico-political process.

To escape from the present dead-end, it is necessary for every country to design a transition strategy towards socially equitable, ecologically prudent and economically efficient development adapted to its particular natural, cultural and socio-political environment. This will lead in practice to a plurality of development paths which, it is to be hoped, will be made mutually compatible through discussions at the international level aimed at avoiding conflicts and, whenever possible, actually creating synergies.

A central element in the design of such a transition strategy is to have an idealized vision of the future capable of creating a fair measure of national consensus, in other words the formulation of a 'national project' responding to at least the following two sets of questions:

- What kind of State, what markets, what roles for civil society, and for what goals of development?
- What forms of democratic regulation for different modalities of 'mixed economy' capable of ensuring a civilized (as distinct from barbarous or savage) growth?

Both in his academic and in his political activity, Cristovam Buarque is deeply committed to the endeavour with respect to his own country, Brazil. In his writings, in his public speeches, in his attempts at restructuring the University of Brasília, this preoccupation with a national project has always been present, manifesting itself through innovative and often provocative approaches.

The present book stems from the same inspiration. It constitutes a sort of theoretical prolegomenon to the formulation of a national project for Brazil and, much more widely, to the reorientation of economics inself as a discipline. Buarque's ideas are often polemical, but always stimulating. Hence the interest of this book.

Ignacy Sachs
Paris

Preface

In 1980, I was on an assignment in Manaus, one of the most sweltering and wretched of Brazil's big cities, in the steaming heart of the Amazon jungle. In the midst of a traffic jam, the chauffeur of the car I was in drew my attention to a young man streaming with sweat, sealed up in a sizzling old Volkswagen. The driver commented: 'That young chap keeps the windows of his car closed so people will think it's air-conditioned!'

If one takes an overall view of Brazil, with its dazzling industrialization as well as its daunting social misery, it takes no great gift of perception to see that the country's one hundred and fifty million inhabitants behave much like the VW owner: we keep our windows clamped shut so that the outside world will take us for a developed country.

For that young man, as for Brazilians generally, economic development did not lie in the power to control his immediate environment but rather in possessing (or feigning to possess) the technology that would grant him such power, even though he might stifle as a result. Social objectives have been subordinated and viewed as a consequence of technical progress rather than as the purpose of civilization. Ethical values, meanwhile, have been discarded.

In 1966, I graduated in Mechanical Engineering in the belief that this was the best way to build the industrial utopia that would rid Brazil of its poverty. I soon realized that the eradication of poverty and the establishment of a utopia required an *economic* rationale that could hold sway over and above the realm of technology. It was this outlook that led me to study for a doctorate in Economics at the Sorbonne, and then to devote long years of service in Latin America and the United States to both theoretical and practical assessment of the economic and social aspects of projects, both as an employee of the Inter-American Development Bank and as a consultant for a number of international agencies, especially those attached to the United Nations.

It eventually dawned on me, however, that subordinating technical imperatives to an economic rationale would also not suffice. True development demands not only understanding and mastering the most efficient means of accomplishing progress but also, at a more profound level, a capacity to define the very purposes that should be sought. This implies subverting the traditional view of progress as simply the equivalent of the techniques employed. It is, indeed, essential that technology be subordinate to an economic rationale, but this must, in turn, be circumscribed by social objectives which must ultimately be dictated by ethical values.

Just as Physics stumbled upon the need for regulatory ethics the moment it became aware of its catastrophic potential, so Economics sorely needs to rediscover ethics. The present dilemma will not be dispelled merely by re-evaluating the means and totting up new costs – as one does in project assessment. Rather, it is a matter of changing the core objectives of the social process, delivering it from the econo-mistic straitjacket of the last two centuries.

Without subverting the traditional notion of progress, it will be impossible to grapple with the problem of growing poverty and inequality, and impossible to incorporate ecological balance into social purposes. The issue of economic development thus demands a fresh theoretical approach founded on three pillars: an ethics for re-defining the very objectives of civilization; a new definition of the object and field of study, capable of taking in the ecological dimension; and a new rationale for Economics as a discipline.

These convictions were gradually worked out in the process of teaching courses on Economic Development at Brasília University and eventually took the shape of a book entitled *The Disorder of Progress*, published in 1990. The book has been very well received in academic circles and by the general reading public in Brazil.

In 1992, during a course held at Thames Polytechnic (now Greenwich University), I expanded on these ideas, extending the conundrum of the crisis of economic thinking beyond the scope of a country like Brazil to a global scale. I pondered on the fact that economic growth has not brought the world the utopia it had expected and hankered after. On the contrary, the world now seems headed for a clear-cut social division which may, in a matter of centuries (decades even), lead to the establishment of two distinct 'species' of human beings.

Comparing our present world at the close of this century with the dreams men cherished a hundred years ago, one could claim that civilization has accomplished and surpassed all their expectations from the point of view of power and technical know-how. It is the uses to which this power and knowledge have been put that have led us away from Utopia. Nor has Economics been a failure: its very success has brought about the present crisis of civilization.

In physical, cultural and even political terms, the dream of an integrated world has virtually been fulfilled, but, alas, coupled to a growing social divide between people. There is political, economic, social and cultural integration among those who are party to modernity, whichever country they may inhabit, North or South, while the gaping rift that separates them from the poor yawns wider. It is futile to divide us into First and Third Worlds because the distinction is not one of countries but of social classes. The rich and middle classes in averagely poor countries are often better off than the rich and the middle class in averagely rich ones. The integrated world has built not a marvellous Planetary First World but a menacing Giant Third World. Sociologically speaking, Planet Earth is of the Third World breed. It is not a matter of harping on the conflict between rich and poor countries, but of coming to terms with an integrated planet where people are segregated between the elect and the outcasts, regardless of national boundaries.

The ecological crisis demonstrates that the level of consumption among the rich cannot be extended to the entire population of the globe. The rich, the world over, are marching to implement a form of apartheid: Brazilians by fencing themselves off from the surrounding misery in guarded condominiums; West Europeans by spurning immigrants from East and South; North Americans by impounding Haitians in refugee camps; the whole world by its indifference to the plight of the boat people.

We stand at a crossroads: either we blunder on in a doomed search for a brand of development geared to universal consumption and technology, building up a system of social partitioning on a global scale; or else we branch off onto fresh ground by accepting the challenge to build a new order in which the economic system is governed by ethical principles, a framework in which respect for nature and abolition of human want would be the key social objectives to be pursued and accomplished.

The lack of a planet-wide social understanding of the situation confronting humanity and the non-existence of mechanisms for international political participation thwart the effectiveness of instruments designed to regulate the use of technology, whose power reaches way beyond national frontiers. Being able to survey the future from the vantage-point of countries like Brazil is thus an opportunity to be seized. The Third World is no longer limited to underdeveloped countries; the whole planet is becoming a global Third World.

The challenge facing present-day Brazil is the same as that facing the planet: either we build an apartheid society, addicted to consumption for a minority, that destroys the environment and treats its excluded masses in an authoritarian manner, or else we invent a brave new future that embraces the whole of humanity, one located in a natural cosmos to be valued in its own right.

This is the debate that the present book attempts to address.

Cristovam Buarque

Note on the Translation

This book has been translated from Portuguese by Dr Mark Ridd. While based on a book written originally by the author, Cristovam Buarque, in Portuguese and published under the title *A Desordem do Progresso*, the English language edition was heavily revised by the author in the process of being translated and, in addition, includes one completely new concluding chapter.

CHAPTER 1

The Need for Ethics

The evolution of science and ethics

In *Science and Human Values*, Jacob Bronowski says that he first became clearly aware of humankind the day he set foot in Nagasaki, just three months after the explosion of the atom bomb: 'For the moment ... was a universal moment; what I met was, almost as abruptly, the experience of mankind.'

What he felt at that instant was a sharp awakening from a 2,500-year-long slumber during which Physics had evolved at the expense of a constant, systematic erosion of the ethics that had underpinned and expressed the will of the gods.

When they set about formulating their explanation of the world, the first physicists brushed aside the explanations handed down to them through myths and beliefs. In their place, they proffered their own perception of reality, filtered by an instrument that seemed neutral enough to them: their capacity to think logically. From then on, every inch science advanced meant a retreat on the part of the mythical set of ethical values hitherto used to explain the world. Science evolved through disenchantment, which involved weeding out the divine from explanations of reality. Rational models freed the explanation of things from the bonds of the mythical beliefs that underpinned previous explanations. Scientific thinking allowed ideas to shed the ethics governing prevailing explanations, in which the hand of good and bad gods was seen in every sunrise and sunset, in eclipses and earthquakes, and was deemed to be behind the creation and operation of the world.

In attempting to explain the behaviour of the heavens, scientists like Galileo, Kepler and Newton did away with the myths, visions and value judgements by which people had traditionally described how the gods employed celestial bodies as instruments of their ethical designs. In so doing, science did not merely abolish ethics; it stumbled upon the logic that was to shape scientific thinking. The progress of science thus depended on human conscience breaking free from the ethical values that had thus far explained the world.

This process was taken still further as purely explanatory science attained a degree of technological power that could provoke ever-increasing transformation. This continued until the day when technological power put the very future of the world in peril and began to instil dread in humankind as a whole.

Even physicists who did not see the devastation wreaked by the atom bomb first hand were shocked by this evidence of the awesome power of the science and technology they handled. The shattering impact of the atom bomb threw into clear relief the responsibility not only of those who had decided to use it but also of those who had conceived, developed and produced it.

It was the full weight of this responsibility that struck Bronowski as he surveyed the mounds of rubble to which Nagasaki had been reduced. As a physicist, he became suddenly and acutely aware of the sheer destructive power of the energy that the human race had learnt to harness. It was then that the need for regulatory ethics dawned on him – the ethics of god-like humans supplanting the ethics of their gods. Physics had come full circle in abolishing explanatory ethics; a new regulatory ethics was now required.

The same path has since been trodden by several other sciences, following precisely the same logical footsteps, though the time taken to complete the circuit has varied. Each science has passed through three distinct phases: an initial one, in which it simply explains phenomena, replacing the prevalent ethical-deistic explanation; a second phase, in which it acquires power to transform, yet still without the need for any form of ethical buttressing; and a third phase, when its power to transform attains such catastrophic proportions that scientists become aware of the need for a new kind of ethical behaviour to regulate their actions.

Astronomers, unlike nuclear physicists, feel no need for regulatory ethics. Since Astronomy is as yet a purely explanatory science, it is devoted to abolishing ethics as a source of explanation for the phenomena of the cosmos. Discovering the laws of the universe, Astronomy acquires scientific legitimacy as it progressively does away with mythical explanations. Like Newton three hundred years ago, astronomers need feel no apprehension about the use to which their equations for the movement of celestial bodies are put. As astronomical knowledge evolves, however, associated with advances in other scientific fields, and celestial engineering comes into being, astronomers will acquire the power of intervention. Even then, so long as their power is restricted to tiny asteroids, society will be able to feel at ease in the company of innocent astronomers. Should their power expand, though, to the point where they can manipulate gravitational forces and thus ring changes in celestial architecture, the need for regulatory ethics will at once arise.

This assertion of the essential place of ethics in science does not mean a return to the mythical past. Rather, it should be seen as an advance in our understanding of the role of science and its increasing power to transform reality. It encapsulates the need to instil moral values into the uses to which such power is put. It is, then, a means of steering clear of mysticism while continuing to foster humanism.

This is where the contradiction between the acquisition of knowledge and the moral utilization of such knowledge surfaces.

We no longer need to resort to myths to explain or regulate the use of our knowledge, but this does not mean that we can spurn belief in human values. We must now develop or reveal new regulatory values for controlling the way knowledge is exploited. Scientists will not be forgoing independent thought, but they will be relinquishing a certain independence in the application of their knowledge with regard to other people and to God, both of whom are necessary for legitimating the bounds that may come to limit the power of scientists to act.

At the outset, lulled into a sense of security by the yawning chasm separating theoretical knowledge from any real possibility of producing the bomb, Nuclear Physics was tolerant of this contradiction. In 1921, Einstein confided to a young disciple that he could not afford to waste precious time developing a weapon based on his $E = m.c^2$ formula.[1] He reckoned it was virtually impossible to produce one. The great physicist did not then feel compelled to play the pacifist he was later to become, for at that point the power of science to transform was not plainly apparent.

Even when the potential use of pure Physics began to take concrete shape at the hands of technology, Einstein was willing to participate in this development and to encourage research that might lead to the production of the bomb – to his mind, an answer to the threat posed by Fascism. An ethics for regulating the use of the bomb was a natural requirement. Scientists, indeed, felt comfortably protected since their discoveries could only be put to practical use with the consent of democratic societies. They entrusted politicians with the responsibility for deciding the fate of their feats of genius, granting themselves the luxury of ethical exemption from whatever consequences their theories might have.

This sense of coddled exemption melted away the moment they realized the consequences of dropping the atom bomb. Most physicists then began to wake up to the responsibility that rested upon their shoulders. What changed in 1945 was not the magnitude of the crime but the degree of fear and horror it aroused. The use of science for war was not new, but the extent of the impact that science could cause was a chilling novelty.[2]

Progress in other areas in the second half of the 20th century has led sciences other than Physics to encounter the need for regulatory ethics. After centuries of maintaining a neutral stance, physicists, biologists and chemists are increasingly displaying concern for ethics, both in their research and also with regard to its by-products. Biologists strive to anticipate the potential effects of genetic engineering and express a concern for regulatory ethics; genetic engineers are aware that, despite its fabulous potential, their research may produce catastrophic results; engineers are sensitive to the way robotics may affect levels of employment; agronomists worry about the side-effects of pesticides; information technologists (ranging from those working on microelectronics to those engaged in producing computer systems) are beginning to consider the moral implications of their work. In the medium and long run, as it permeates society, information technology may demand standardization and thus require control mechanisms that would 'spontaneously' curb individual freedom for the sake of social efficiency.

When microelectronics joins forces with genetic engineering and modern neurosurgery, it will be within our grasp to create mutating species of individuals whose potential could upset the balance between people and between nations. Just as the idea of an integrated world begins to be seen as a feasible dream for mankind, awareness is growing of the risk of some biological process creating definitive and insurmountable differences between people at the unwitting hand of science. Already, medicine, nutrition, the use of computers, genetic potential and surgical techniques are leading towards what, in effect, almost amount to different species within the human race.

All this is imbuing modern sciences with an awareness of their potential for upsetting the balance of nature and bringing about changes that may have serious and unpredictable consequences for nature and humanity alike.

It is becoming similarly apparent that laboratories are not entirely capable of controlling their brainchildren. This suggests a need to control the research process itself by establishing strict norms and safety procedures, even at the cost of slackening the pace at which knowledge advances. For those with a finer sense of ethics, this would still leave considerable leeway for scientists to unleash undesirable effects.

There is virtual consensus about the risk of leaving today's scientists to act freely at the prompting of the same spirit of pure scientific curiosity that has prevailed since the Enlightenment. Scientists and technicians realize that they no longer merely explain how the real world operates but have also become agents of its transformation. Their powers now outrun the human and the short term and attain planetary scope and permanence.

After centuries playing *with* God, by extending the horizon of their power to explain, scientists have begun to play *at* God, expanding their power to intervene. This is a game in which it would seem that the more successful science is at explaining the world, the more patently it bears the seeds of its own failure, since the knowledge it generates threatens the very object of its concern. Scientists possess firm knowledge of the means but only a shaky command of the consequences. Unless, that is, they are provided with standards dictated by ethical values.

The reason why the very success of science harbours the germ of its failure would appear to be the fact that the reasoning that sustains it – applied to controlling the reality of the physical world – has evolved much faster than the urge to define the purposes of the control that we (as social beings) exert on reality. What has emerged is a science that progresses due to the global nature of its explanations and power, while society continues to operate on the basis of individual or, at most, national urges. We have harnessed the power to wreak planetary destruction but have failed to forge a planetary consciousness.

According to Arthur Koestler in *Jano: A Summing Up*, this situation arises because the efficiency-geared, reasoning side of the human brain tends to develop faster than its emotional counterpart. We are thus the only schizophrenic species, and the only species whose extinction may be induced by endogenous actions, constituting a form of suicide.[3] It is worth remembering that Koestler begins his book by saying that if he had to pick the most important watershed in the history of the human race, he would settle for 6 August 1945: 'The reason is simple. From the dawning of human consciousness to the 6th of August, 1945, man had to come to terms with the prospect of his death as an individual. Since the day the first atom bomb outshone the sun in Hiroshima, mankind as a whole has had to live with the prospect of its extinction as a species.' It is interesting that Koestler did not refer to 16 July 1945, when the first experimental atomic explosion was carried out at Los Alamos in New Mexico. Up to that point, the bomb was basically a product of a single side of the brain, hatched in the chill light in which reason probes and manipulates the world. It is on 6 August 1945, however, that the aesthetics of reason makes way for the emotional side that implements the power generated by the rational half of the brain. One side acquires the new power to manipulate nature, the other manipulates this power, driven by sentiments as ancient as the human race itself.

It is at the precise instant when the two halves of the single but divided brain clash that our schizophrenic imbalance surfaces. The human brain is capable of elaborate mental processes that unveil and explore the intimate recesses of the invisible atom, yet it is immature enough not to be able to douse the simmering primary conflicts that lead to wars – a curious mix of emotion and logic, bereft of a higher reason holding the two in harmonious balance.

Perhaps Einstein's reaction at being informed, while on holiday, that the bomb had been dropped on Hiroshima was best. He said candidly: 'The world was not yet ready.' Nor had it been ready for the test explosion on 16 July 1945. It had not even been prepared for his theory postulating that energy and matter were two different manifestations of the same entity, and that simply transforming one into the other would cause a mighty bang. So long as it remained a formula, or a spectacular fireworks display, the world would look on in wonder. It would also observe the explosion with a good deal less fear if the detonation were to occur after sufficient evolution of the emotional side of our primitive instincts. But that, of course, is not how events transpired. The bomb was let loose by brains still torn between their advanced and primitive halves.

However, in contrast to Koestler's pessimistic outlook (which later led him to suicide) and to Einstein's concerned, sceptical attitude, it is possible to believe that the destructive power of science may arouse in humankind an awareness of the need for ethics to control its use. The very strength of science is rousing our emotions and reason to consciousness of the need for control.

There are good reasons for believing in the feasibility of a swift advance in the quest for such ethics. A hallmark of today's world is the steady growth in concern for the balance of nature. There is a burgeoning quest to develop means of protecting the human race against nuclear war.

Unfortunately, such moves have so far been but timid, though there would seem to be a trend towards dynamic growth. Worse still, they have met with only a lukewarm reception from social scientists.

The failure of the social sciences

There is as yet no sign of a generalized concern, like that shown by physicists, blossoming in the social sciences. The atom bomb had such a devastating and instantaneous impact that it awakened in physicists an awareness that slow social process has not yet managed to instil in social scientists as they fly over territories and cities laid waste by the economics of a savage form of development, implemented by deliberate technological formulations.

Even more serious, social scientists, unlike physicists, have not managed to pin down a precise notion of creation or destruction. Whereas for almost all physicists (and according to the dictates of common sense) the explosion of an atom bomb suggests destruction, for social scientists the large-scale burning of the Amazon forest or the impoverishment of the masses may simply be part of the avowedly positive process of development. Almost all economists view this process as some physicists once viewed the explosion of the atom bomb: as a battle necessary for ultimate victory. Indeed, some social scientists reckon their role is merely to analyse and explain, free from any responsibility to intervene and administer the social process. Just like the physicists who developed the atom bomb and the bomber pilots who dropped it, these social scientists feel they are only doing their job, without the power or the onus to take decisions. For them, the role they play is aesthetic, part of the beauty of knowledge and technological prowess. The ethics of decision-making is a lot that falls to the politicians.

Finally, social scientists still seem slightly dazzled by the knowledge they have only recently begun to amass. Quite unlike physicists – who have been advancing towards the abolition of myths for the last 2,500 years, and are already bitten by curiosity about the value of the application of their knowledge – social scientists are only just beginning to work out explanations for the behaviour of societies, and stand amazed at the power they have acquired.

Social scientists still cherish the blissful, neutral stance adopted by social philosophers in the 17th and 18th centuries, who sought merely to explain the workings of society. No power derived from this knowledge, which was confined to obeying norms that satisfied moral precepts and religious dogma. Until the Enlightenment, social philosophers functioned as instruments of explanation, capable of keeping those who contravened the ethical canons established by religion on the straight and narrow path.

The thinkers of the Enlightenment, especially Adam Smith, attempted to lay the foundations of knowledge that could legitimize the new behavioural demands of the incipient Industrial Revolution. At the same time, they sought to provide explanations for the social process with the same independence, neutrality and refinement displayed by physicists since the Renaissance, particularly Newton. There was a show of intention to apply the neutrality of physical sciences to social phenomena, while none the less maintaining a subordinate commitment to the ethical premises of nascent capitalism. So, while physicists busied themselves in elaborating neutral theories about a world that obliged them to be neutral (impotent as they were to control the destiny of things physical), social scientists subscribed and aspired to neutrality in the logical formulation of how the body social operated. They could not, however, bring themselves to forswear voluntary acceptance of the norms and destiny to which society was bound. At any event, they stuck to an explanatory, non-interventionist tack.

The position today is entirely different. Sensitive physicists could not fail to feel deeply disturbed by what they witnessed in Nagasaki, nor to cease viewing the atom bomb as a mere scientific wonder. Social scientists likewise (especially economists) cannot fail to notice the dramatic effects of the development models currently being implemented in Third World countries. If they open their eyes, as Bronowski did, not only will they see the fabulous force of the transformation that has wrought an efficient world, but they will also take stock of the nastier side of the equation: wretchedness that reduces people to scrap on a rubbish tip; cultural domination that bulldozes societies to the verge of insanity; depredation of nature that jeopardizes the future of the human race itself.

In a way, this other bomb may be more dramatic, since the nuclear bomb would naturally produce self-limiting mechanisms. It would initially wipe out the societies that attacked each other, but the remainder of humanity would at least stand a chance of surviving, however deplorable conditions might be. The economic growth bomb, with its silent, subterranean explosions, insidiously deludes each private citizen, and so tends to dissipate any equalizing effects. Unless, that is, society should prove capable of perceiving its consequences and taking steps to bring it under control.

Only in very recent times and to a very limited extent has this uneasiness about the limits to and risks of growth begun to sink into the consciousness of intellectuals and the population at large. Even so, many economists refuse outright to face up to the issue within the domain of science itself.

The abolition of explanatory ethics in Economics

It is only with Adam Smith that the understanding of the economic process begins to acquire legitimacy as part of scientific knowledge. Before Smith, the economist's role was more to legitimize the behaviour of economic agents (under the aegis of the prevailing ideology) than to come to grips with the workings of production and distribution. When necessary, economists also helped to bend ethical rules to make allowance for the advance of technology and socio-economic organization. Myth and Economics were thus fused, as Marvin Harris proposes in his book *Cannibals and Kings: The Origins of Cultures*.[4] According to Harris, religion itself, myths and customs originated in and obeyed the laws of economic logic. To his mind, cannibalism and ritual sacrifices were brought about by scarcity of protein in a particular region, added to the need to justify the privileged consumption of

delicacies by just one select segment of the population. The econo-
mist-priest was entrusted with regulating social action by means of
religious rules subject to an economic rationale.

In a way, this state of affairs has remained unaltered to the present
day. The science of Economics continues to serve as an instrument for
legitimating the behaviour of economic agents, churning out sets of
ideas that can only be justified by cults as weird and illogical as those
of anthropophagic religions.

Anyone not under the spell of the precepts of economic logic can
readily spot the absurdities of modern economies. Capital accumulation through slave labour or the payment of low wages, and income
concentration produced by economic policies, are very real, if dis-
guised, forms of cannibalism. Economists, like Aztec priests,
however, manage to conjure up ways of explaining and justifying each
and every absurdity.

The history of economic thinking illustrates the bond linking society's ethical values, its need for efficient behaviour (from the point of
view of survival) and the explanations put forward by those who have
acted as economists in one way or another.

The Greeks – the first to formulate economic thought in the western
world – moulded their theories in absolute respect for existing custom.
Despite their exceptional sophistication, none of their economic theories repudiated slavery. On the contrary, they worked out schemes for
exploring it to the full. They treated the use of slave labour with such
nonchalance that the concept of work itself did not make it onto their
list of actions worthy of a man. Even Plato, with all his humanism,
excluded slaves and craftsmen from his Greek *polis*, or city. In his
opinion, 'Work remains beyond any human value and, in certain
respects, seems the very antithesis of what is essential to man.'[5]

In the Middle Ages, the subordination of material life to future
spiritual existence in heaven produced economic canons in which the
notion of sin was present in the condemnation of all activities not
strictly coherent with the survival and enrichment of princes and the
church. Charging interest and developing trade beyond bare necessities were declared sinful. The underlying principle of economic
activity and of all labour, as a result, was the same as that governing
the rest of life: the attainment of heaven.

The expansion and progress of trade, however, demanded the
liberalization of ethical principles, which had to adapt to new circum-

stances. This included loosening up the concept of fair prices, permitting the charging of interest, and so on.

After Europe discovered America, and especially in the wake of the settlement of the Caribbean, North-east Brazil and the southern United States, slavery was pushed to its absolute limit as a system of production and administrative sophistication. Huge resources were efficiently mustered to capture, transport, sell and put slaves to work through a vast trading network involving millions of people (either as agents or as merchandise) and millions of pounds, and extending for thousands of miles.

Save for isolated protests from intellectuals and politicians, economists levelled no criticism at slavery. When they did eventually speak out against it, this was because economic process had advanced to the point of making slavery an inefficient method of production. Economists only came round to condemning slavery when modern capitalism began to require new moral attitudes. It was not the humanism of securing freedom for slaves that was at stake, but rather freedom for trade that could most profitably advance capitalist evolution.

It is the Industrial Revolution that frees slaves from bondage – though neither on religious grounds nor at the behest of some worthy ethical principle. For the first time in history, there is widespread acceptance of a rationale not tethered to the need to survive, a rationale not directly related to the immediate needs of the populace. By installing machines, capitalism can dispense with manpower and spawn an army of unemployed labourers who will force down the wages of free men and women, making it cheaper to purchase their labour than to invest in slaves. Moreover, some of these free workers, through having to purchase goods, will form the market that capitalist Economics requires for its continued dynamism.

As it abolishes slavery, the Industrial Revolution's brand of capitalism makes ethical all forms of exploitation that do not imply actually depriving an individual of his or her freedom. This applies just as much to those who exploit (if possible) as to those who are exploited (if need be), providing both parties are freely involved in the transaction. Capitalism likewise unfetters all forms of economic action, making them neutral and therefore ethically licit.

Capitalism disencumbered economic activities, and there thus arose a need for a theory that could legitimize such liberality. In order to steer clear of ethical stumbling blocks, the most practical course was to create a science that would support this neutral stance by dispensing with ethics. This meant adopting a mechanistic approach in which the agents involved (labour and nature) could be treated like the celestial bodies in Newton's mechanics, or like the chemical elements that science was beginning to unearth and submit to mathematical analysis. To this end, laws that could explain how these elements behaved and related to each other needed to be developed: non-ethical laws for explaining a natural movement which, none the less, was made up of human beings, wills, desires, emotions and interests.

It took a professor of ethics to prise the science of Economics from the clutches of ethics – to exclude ethics from the explanation of the economic process. Adam Smith made three important contributions that entitle him to be dubbed the father of Economics. First, he redefined the concept of wealth, adapting it to the reality of the budding capitalist system. Until then, the standard concept of wealth was synonymous with stored-up treasure, particularly precious metals. Economics needed to be set free from this natural fetter so that the wealth of a nation could come to be seen as its power to produce. Secondly, he banished the will of God and of humankind from the logic that explained the workings of the economy. Until Smith, views of Economics as an instrument for accomplishing the designs of the Almighty on earth were rife. Thirdly, he provided an explanation of how the economy actually worked, defining laws by which an 'invisible hand' regulated the process and maintained a constant trend towards equilibrium.

After writing a classic essay on ethics (his *Theory of Moral Sentiments*), Adam Smith set about formulating the bases of the economic theory that was to abolish ethical premises. In their stead, he instituted a philosophy based on neutral, natural laws similar to those that Newton had used to explain the movement of the cosmos one hundred years earlier. In a way, this is what is behind the 'Adam Smith paradox', as Ana Maria Bianchi points out when considering the 'supposed contradiction between his Theory – whose ethical rationale is founded on human sympathy – and his *Wealth of Nations* – which strongly depicts man as being motivated by calculating egoism'.[6] Smith-the-economist made egoism the mainspring of the social process, regardless of any value judgement about this human passion and its consequences. Moral values thus cease to be the guiding principles of human behaviour and become instruments for controlling and rallying economic agents for economic ends, a process Max Weber analyses so well.[7]

From then on, economists managed to rid themselves of the religious precepts and prejudices that had made them the pawns of theologians. All the time, though, they believed in a hand as invisible as that which moved celestial bodies, and so did not bother to intervene. Just as in the physicists' heavens, the economic process obeyed mechanisms and norms imposed by a natural order. The logic of this order was the object of their studies, and they concentrated on explaining it. Science was to be neutral where the behaviour of economic agents was concerned. Like other scientists, economists sought to eliminate value judgements from economic explanations. This was tantamount to proposing a new value judgement: the belief that Economics should neither produce value judgements nor, therefore, possess its own ethics.

This new value judgement is plain to see in the pains economists since Smith have taken to approximate the language explaining economic phenomena to that of Mathematics. They behave as if the incorporation of Mathematics were proof of the elimination of value judgements in explanations of the behaviour of economic agents – as if, by modifying the language of the statement, they could somehow mitigate the criminal's guilt.

Economic thought has thus followed the same path as any other branch of scientific thinking. The Enlightenment outlook prevalent in the western world since the 18th century has enabled scientific thought to be built up through progressive distancing from its respective explanatory ethics. Scientific thought renounced mythical or religious metaphysics to embrace an explanation for reality that transcended value judgements. As in other sciences, the more economic thought progressed, the fewer ethical and speculative elements it should contain.

The 'invisible hand' regulating economic agents' each and every move allayed their ethical misgivings. The sole value of each agent consisted in fulfilling his desire to increase his individual and family consumption in the most ambitious and egoistic manner possible. But this fulfilment was not the fruit of a value judgement since it was defined by natural laws applying to humankind. General equilibrium sufficed to legitimate this behaviour which, given its efficiency, was also ethical. If wages were so low as to make workers disgruntled, they would quit their jobs because they were free agents. The invisible hand would then prompt capitalists to raise the wages they paid. If people preferred to spend their money instead of lending it (as the economy required), capitalists would begin to offer higher interest and so attract savers. On the other hand, if interest rates and wages were high, capitalists would cut back investments and slow the pace of their activities, which would in turn make wages and interest rates drop. All that mattered to economists was to explain these mechanisms and their logic.

The science of Economics did not concern itself with the effects that this ethical liberty might have on the lives of millions of people – on workers and the unemployed. No one need care about hunger rubbing shoulders with ostentatious affluence. The scientist's merit was to disengage himself from such prickings of conscience.

It made no difference if economic logic implied accumulation of wealth in the hands of a privileged few provided with abundant cheap labour because survival forced workers to pawn the only merchandise they possessed. It was therefore possible to claim that one class exploited the other. But this exploitation should not be deemed anti-ethical or unethical since it was regulated by market forces – by the invisible hand. The neutrality espoused in the days of slavery was preserved but with a different bias. As long as slavery lasted, there was an ethical justification for it, be it assimilation of enemies and prisoners of war, or the treatment meted out to 'inferior' races. The new economic rationale championed the free market as the bedrock of economic activity. In the market, everything was permissible, thus doing away with the need for non-economic explanations.

The ethics that prized the freedom of each economic agent was built up through the abolition of all other ethical concerns in Economics. The economic 'point of view' came to be expressed within a framework in which ethics is incorporated in the form of its own absence.

Adam Smith was not alone in propounding this epistemological strategy. The leap forward made by Hume, Locke and other leading contemporary social philosophers consisted in dissociating the new social science from the ethical outlook confining it to the realm of social philosophy.

Even when he openly criticizes the exploitation of one person by another, Marx does so without resorting to ethical arguments. Instead, he analyses the structure and destiny of the capitalist system in strictly neutral terms. The novelty of the Marxist explanation is its refusal to incorporate ethical values. Marx simply resolves a logical contradiction in the value-labour theory that Adam Smith and his successors had failed to settle. Marx's notion of exploitation is not an offshoot of his social conscience: it springs from scientific observation. His ethical conscience (wholly committed to the interests of the proletarian masses) may have spurred him to seek an explanation. But when he formulates it, he is looking for an entirely scientific rationale. In the same way, classical economists may have hidden the real face of exploitation on account of their ethical commitment to the ruling classes, but in formulating their explanations they actually offered an alternative form of scientific knowledge.

Marx did not see his explanation of the theory of exploitation as deriving from an ethical presupposition of social justice. Rather, it issued from the discovery – provided by real observation – that workers did not receive the total value of the goods they produced. Until then, economists had not explained just how capitalism appropriated part of the fruits of labour. Ricardo formulated the notion that capitalists were the proprietors of 'dead labour', kept on ice in the capacity of machines. Marx stripped away this artificial excuse by simply recalling that, if the labour were dead, it had previously belonged to some worker. There was thus a transference of value from workers to capitalists. He called it 'exploitation' because that was the most suitable, the most *scientific* way to describe reality.

The difference between Marx and Ricardo is not to be found in ethical values. Ricardo had no desire to take a close look at this aspect of reality because the definition of exploitation betrayed his class interests, which clashed with his ethical presuppositions. The ethical values of both were ideological frameworks, reflecting their culture and interests. In terms of Economics, both were equally neutral. By clearly demonstrating how the process worked, they could claim to be scientific.

The endeavour to write off ethics in Economics becomes all the more patent when one observes the dynamics of capitalism as Marx saw it. In his opinion, the fragility of capitalism did not consist in the ethical contradiction inherent in exploitation but rather in its instrinsic technical characteristics as a system. It was not just the rebellion of the proletarian masses against the system that exploited them that indicated the non-viability of capitalism. The eventual decay of capitalism was unavoidable because the system bore a logic that made it unfeasible in the long run. By deducting from workers part of the value of the goods they produced, the system necessarily created output without end-buyers. The battle for a limited market, added to the need to raise output, would generate a feud between capitalists. They would then resort to increasing the quantity of capital as a means of cutting costs and prices. This would inevitably lead to a constant reduction in profits which, after successive crises, would tend towards zero. Technical advances would provide productivity gains, but the market is restrained by such advances. The problem is a technical one, determined by the laws of historical materialism, not by the conscience of humanist ethics. Even the proletariat's position at the forefront of the endeavour to free people from bondage derives from its being engaged in a political struggle to defend its class interests, driven by awareness of its own exploitation, and not by humanist conscience.

This outlook is reinforced by the first generation of neo-classical economists who, spurning Marx's considerations, strove to advance on the ideas of Adam Smith. This is when the science of Economics enters the second stage. In this phase it dumps ethics for good by explaining in detail how each economic action is linked in a general equilibrium formulated on mathematical principles. Economics begins to aspire to the status of sciences that have achieved neutral mathematical methods of explaining reality.

With the neo-classical school, the Industrial Revolution liberates economic science from explanatory ethical values.[8]

Interventionist Economics

In the 20th century, from the 1930s onwards, the science of Economics abandons its purely explanatory role and assumes a technological function, intervening in the social process. Until then, the pamphleteers and mercantilist consultants – or economists like Ricardo in the 19th century – had very specific objectives, concentrating on the nuts and bolts of humdrum problems. No one ever dreamt of tampering with the overall workings of the machinery of the economic system.

With Keynes, behaviour in relation to intervention changes but the posture of hypothetical ethical neutrality remains unaltered. Successive crises (which actually largely confirmed Marx's theoretical formulations) convinced Keynes of the need for, and viability of, state intervention as the only means of compensating for the invisible hand's inability to maintain the necessary balance. It is symptomatic that Keynes' first important study was on the negative consequences of the end of the First World War – examined from an entirely non-ethical point of view. His was not a problem of ethical or aesthetic values but of technical actions. In the absence of an explanation based on ethical values, one can conclude that peace is a problem for human society since it brings economic stagnation as a backlash. It is almost as if Bronowski, on visiting Nagasaki, had lamented Japan's surrender because of the slow-down it would produce in the manufacture of new bombs.

When they realize that the invisible hand setting divine norms requires nudging, economists start interfering in its designs. They continue to feel that there is no worry about the course that has been plotted, thanks to their induction. Economists are catapulted from the supporting role of interpreters to star as God's partners – though destitute of a greater concern for the consequences or purposes of their actions.

Both former neutral stances (on theoretical analysis and on non-intervention), though coherent in themselves, start to contradict each other the moment they are united. This makes theory foster intervention. Though they may maintain lip service to ethical neutrality, economists are no longer neutral once they intervene in reality. This is true for both the natural order they have modified and, even more, for the new order they have helped to usher in.

In Keynes' case, this contradiction can be explained. Within his ideological limits, the measures he proposed benefited all classes – though the benefits were unequal – since they restored the level of employment of all the production factors involved. Under this ideological umbrella, Keynesian economists either failed to notice or turned a blind eye to the fact (already announced by Malthus and denounced by Marx) that these proposals demand wars, unproductive labour in digging and filling in holes in the ground or erecting pyramids, and other instances of irrational behaviour. The economist, like the physicist who designs an atom bomb, does no more than indicate technical solutions. The politicians are left to undertake the thorny task of opting for war (or an atmosphere of war) to reinstate the desired balance.

This state of affairs becomes all the more contradictory after the Second World War, when Keynesian instruments are employed to stimulate the development of 'backward countries'. Once it became clear that one could intervene to restore equilibrium in an economy, economists realized that they could also tamper with the paralysing inertia of stagnant economies by means of what came to be known as economic development strategies.

It was thus no longer a case of helping the invisible hand to keep society on its road to development. Rather, it was a case of intervening to change course, to build new societies out of 'backward economies' by means of artificial dynamics.

Once again, and in a much more dramatic fashion, science resorts to intervention and lays aside neutrality in relation to reality and local cultural values. Yet, all the while, it preserves a neutral attitude in its dealings with the results produced. Economists start managing whole societies with the sole objective of achieving growth in economic output, neglecting all other factors including the non-economic costs this entails. This is because they possess no ethical rationale to match the greater designs of a humanist project for civilization.

This over-simplified view of economists as a uniform group is clearly unrealistic. One can distinguish a wide range of different trends that can be grouped into three basic schools:

(1) Neo-classical economists, in the guise of modern monetarists, who still espouse non-interventionist observation, confining their action to measures for fine-tuning the economy. They only countenance intervention in politics: police states conveniently keep unions and the masses under tight control to avoid generating imbalances that 'excessive' wage claims and demands for employment might otherwise create.

(2) Orthodox Marxist economists, who concentrate on critical analysis of the capitalist structure and defend the radical global transformation of society. Central planning, they believe, wards off crises, providing growing output and equitable distribution of the proceeds at the same time.

(3) Keynes' followers (some of whom present Marxist overtones in their analyses), who have no qualms about intervening in the economy in order to achieve efficient modern capitalism.

None of these schools places a proper emphasis on the ethical values they should serve. Unlike Bronowski in 1945, most economists today still feel proud as Punch of the results of their labours over the last three decades. After all, their intervention has treated developed economies to a previously unimaginable period of consumption (crises being kept to a minimum) and has enabled Third World economies to attain high rates of growth in output. The crises that have cropped up *en route* are not imputed to the economic decisions themselves. It is as if they derived from the fractiousness of the agents involved: workers who demand too much; Arabs who raise oil prices too high; the earth that is too slow at recycling pollution.

Their sense of exemption has three explanations. First, because even when they play God as social engineers, economists refrain from discussing economic purposes. They are arrogant and pretentious in their handling of the means but reserved when it comes to discussing the value of the ends. Secondly, because they assume that there are no limits to the expansion of an increasingly consumption-oriented society. Thirdly, because the resulting imbalances, such as poverty, are treated as passing phenomena that will right themselves in due course, as the measures employed take effect. It never occurs to them that these imbalances have been brought on by such measures. They stolidly believe that intervention will snap the economy out of inertia, and that the general equilibrium can be restored by natural means.

Nevertheless, as the 20th century draws to a close, unblinkered observation of reality is at last beginning to sow deep doubts in the minds of many economists.

Precisely as in other sciences, the very success of Economics is gradually revealing its limitations. Growth has led to existential crises in developed countries. The symptoms can be detected in high levels of pollution, consumption of chemical drugs and addiction to the economic drugs of consumption, as well as an ecologically destabilizing production system as far as the availability of natural resources is concerned. In developing countries, growth has heightened dependence, inequality and instability at all levels, while also provoking the same ecological imbalances experienced in rich countries. The yawning chasm dividing countries off into opposing camps has widened still further in this world governed by a blatantly unstable economic order.

Far from reckoning this to spell the end of the line for Economics, we should stress the need for regulatory ethics. Such ethics must impose limits and standards on science. Unlike Physics, however, where ethics is seen as an external regulating mechanism, in Economics ethics must be incorporated as part of its very essence, marrow and lifeblood.

Notes

1. Quoted in Ronald C. Clark's *Einstein: The Life and Times*, New York, Avon, 1971, p. 135.

2. C. Buarque, 'Six Wars and One Peace', *IPRA Review*, 1987.

3. See Arthur Koestler, *Jano: A Summing Up*, London, Hutchinson, 1978.

4. Marvin Harris, *Cannibals and Kings: The Origins of Cultures*, New York, Vintage Books, 1977.

5. See J.P. Vermant, *Mythe et Pensée chez les Grecs*, Paris, 1965, pp. 192-217, quoted in Perry Anderson, *Passages from Antiquity to Feudalism*, London, Verso/New Left Books, 1974.

6. Ana Maria Bianchi, *A Pré-história da Economia: De Maquiavel a Adam Smith*, São Paulo, Hucitec, 1988, p. 104.

7. Max Weber, *A Ética Protestante e o Espírito do Capitalismo*, São Paulo, Pioneira, 1967. See also R. Hookaas, *A Religião e o Desenvolvimento da Ciênica Moderna*, Brasília, Ed. Universidade de Brasília, 1988.

8. This becomes clear when one reads a wide-ranging book like Israel Kirzner's *The Economic Point of View*, Mission (Kansas), Sheed & Ward Inc., 1960, in which the problem of ethics is flatly ignored.

CHAPTER 2

The Quest for Essentials

A science among sciences

The sciences have been organized into two entirely separate camps dealing with humankind and nature. In Zoology, and in some branches of Medicine, people are viewed as natural beings but are not examined in their social context. In Anthropology, Sociology, Economics and Psychiatry, on the other hand, they are studied as social beings with no regard for their relation to nature. Natural sciences ignore the power of the human race to create, transform and destroy nature. Other sciences, meanwhile, pay no heed to the possibility of nature having a decisive influence on the destiny of humankind.[1]

The sum total of human knowledge has been carved up between sciences that study the structures and behaviour of minerals, plants and animals, and sciences that study the logic of human behaviour and the material and cultural output of the human race. No science has devoted itself to explaining the logic of the transformation of minerals, plants and animals into people and their products.

This severance of the sciences stems from the sense of self-importance which severed the human race from nature when the process of civilization was consolidated. The arrogance with which Western civilization brandishes its belief in the all-powerful human race, moulded in the image and likeness of God, has had a strong hand in this development.

The science of Economics – which should be closest to integrating humanity and nature – also fails to unite them. Economic theories have tended to view the world from a social standpoint. Even when the natural basis of the economic process is examined, it is classed as 'natural resources'. Such natural resources are only fit to come into existence when people take possession of them (by technological and legal means), absorbing them into the realm of social concerns. Nature, in the pure sense, is deemed to consist solely of minerals, plants and animals - worthless, the lot of them, until appropriated and made to serve as mines, plantations or livestock. Worthless, for the simple reason that they do not contain human labour, according to classical and Marxist theorists alike. And worthless because they do not possess any subjective value which, to the minds of neo-classical theorists, would issue from human consciousness on account of the needs and demands that social relations provoke. What is lacking in both cases is a broader view of the natural process, one that contains the economic process with all its specific features.[2]

Few attempts have been made to reverse this trend and to blend these two distinct approaches in the sciences. And what few attempts have been made have been roundly rejected by Malthus' simplistic vision or spurned by St Francis of Assisi's ideal of spirituality. The lack of scientific objectivity has spelt the demise of both, as has the success of technical advances that have enabled us to offset the natural limitations Malthus envisaged.

Even Marx, who had a strong philosophical concern for nature, refused to ascribe it any economic value in itself. Marx's position is clearly portrayed in Alfred Schmidt's *Marx's Concept of Nature* and Rodrigo A. de Paiva Duarte's *Marx e a Natureza em O Capital*.[3]

In the last twenty years, three discoveries have brought about a change in this situation: in the ideological sphere, the realization that the results of development no longer satisfy consumers; in the ecological sphere, the realization (registered by instruments very different from those Malthus employed) that there are natural limits to economic growth; in the political sphere, the realization that it is not feasible to sustain growing inequality between those progress benefits and those whom it passes by.

All three observations, it should be said, are founded on relatively subjective premises. The various existential movements criticize consumer society on two counts: for the sense of emptiness and boredom it instils, and for the contradictions between the urge to consume and an instrinsic quest for happiness. By placing limits on growth, one assumes that scientific and technological revolutions will not manage to keep pace with unbridled production in replenishing the planet's stock of natural resources. The exhaustion of political solutions is an attitude based on the rejection of the methods employed by societies espousing apartheid.

There are, however, good reasons for claiming that such concerns have objective grounds. In the political arena, there are ethical reasons for rejecting apartheid that do not derive from purely personal outlooks and tastes. There is logic in the very need for solidarity and

co-operation between people. This is equally true of the social framework, without which our first material victories over nature, the
emergence of culture and especially the progress of civilization, would
never have occurred. Co-operation is thus an essential requirement for
social advancement. On the other hand, the cost of sustaining an
unco-operative global society demonstrates that there is no future for
the apartheid model of civilization. Colonial struggles (both on the
international chessboard and in the case of domestic strife in divided
nations) are proving increasingly costly.

On the ecological front, there is nothing to justify the optimistic
hope that scientific and technological progress will suddenly come up
with substitutes for current resources and clean up the environment.
In the foreseeable future, the speed at which environmental depredation and the plundering of natural resources take place could clearly
be greater than the pace at which techniques advance. The growing
costs of technical solutions and the consequent failure to keep costs
down are also plain to see. The size of the hole in the ozone layer, the
tracts of felled forest in the Amazon, the polluted rivers in Europe, the
depletion of oil and gas reserves, the repeated leakages and spillages
(of radioactive material in Chernobyl and oil in Alaska) – all these
take place far more rapidly than any foreseeable spontaneous change
in consumption levels or technological modifications in industrial
energy generation, let alone an about-turn in the urge to make quick
personal profit. Should economic growth and technical advances
proceed at their present breakneck speed, there is every indication that
we are headed for saturation in industrial production as sources of
some raw materials run dry and the environment becomes increasingly
polluted.[4]

Finally, where ideology is concerned, there are solid grounds for
believing that the values of industrial society are in the throes of a
dramatic crisis. What we are witnessing is no longer merely the natural
discontent voiced by minorities. The ecological movement has already evolved beyond minority status and begun to permeate our
collective consciousness – though to a greater extent, obviously,
among young people, more socially coherent groups and the more
well-off. In all three groups, the value of the future is clearer than in
segments of society blinkered by their uphill struggle to survive and
among individualist groups afflicted by temporal short-sightedness.[5]
Urban violence and drug-addiction are no longer simply instances of

warped individual behaviour or group fads; they have spread to the point of becoming clear social pathologies.

What alters the realization of such a state of affairs in a period of crisis is the fact that there is no sign that Economics will bow down to the evidence of ecological catastrophes or that the urge to consume will be spontaneously curbed. Despite sporadic initiatives in particular countries, industries and corporations, there is no general revolution that will deliver clean industry accompanied by high levels of recycling to be glimpsed on the short-term horizon. Nor are there any heartening advances in substituting basic inputs for energy generation, or in industrial and agricultural transformation processes. On the other hand, many people's former conviction that the crisis was restricted to the economic sphere and did not encompass our civilizational model has been steadily undermined in recent decades. The belief that the socialist system was the natural solution for getting civilization back on the rails has also wilted. The splitting of socialism into absolutely opposing factions, the repressed desire to consume in Eastern Europe, and the left's new-found willingness to recognize the political failings of its régimes have revealed that socialism as currently conceived is still committed to an ideology that disdains nature, consolidated during the Industrial Revolution.

The solution will have to be born at a higher level of understanding, one that fuses the reasoning of natural sciences and the logic of the social and human sciences. It must be an all-encompassing form of reasoning: a logic that defines the rationale of the transformation of nature into the human race and its products.

It is not a matter of refuting our central position in the universe – of being foolish or hypocritical enough to deny the foremost importance of civilization in order to defend nature by propounding the idea of life on earth as a single organism, devoid of all distinctions. But neither should we ignore the short span of our history and its fragility when compared to the vast complex of life on earth. Nature should be admired not only for its economic role but also for its beauty – both because, if it were to vanish, the link sustaining human life would be snapped, and because it is a vital part of our heritage.

Rather, it is a matter of justifying our position at the centre, and of understanding the logic that subordinates the economic process, science and technology to ethical principles according to which nature is also a subject of the process that transforms it into our material and cultural products. This ideological revolution will engender a new outlook in our dealings with the 'human enterprise', as it has been considered since the Greeks – a venture termed *civilization* (in a broader sense) or *development* (in a more limited sense).

This revolution will spring from a social process to which all will have contributed their fears and reflections. One can, however, already envisage an outline of this new concept. It will be based on a logic founded on a single guiding principle and grounded in three areas of scientific concern which rationalize the process by which minerals, plants and animals are transformed into and by humankind.

The guiding principle is that the process of civilization should be powered by the constant quest to roll back the horizon of human liberty. There are three components to this quest:

(1) The conquest of more free time, dovetailing with the expansion of the material heritage at society's disposal.

(2) The use of this extra free time for activities associated with the promotion of a diversified and continually growing cultural heritage.

(3) The sharing of this free time between present and future generations, thus permanently preserving nature's productive potential, now viewed as part of civilization's cultural heritage.

It will be necessary to establish a theoretical framework for these forms of knowledge – one that will be submitted to new ethical purposes for civilization, determining an economic rationale compatible with such ethical purposes, and a global approach centred on ecology.

Three forms of knowledge are the bedrock on which this logic must be built: the establishment of an ethical framework for determining the values that are to serve as the guiding principles for broadening the horizon of freedom; an economic theory (subordinate to ethics) to provide a rational means of achieving our objectives; and an ecological approach, subordinating our universe to a permanent state of environmental equilibrium.

Taken together, these three forms of knowledge will form the framework that is to stand as a halfway house between the two separate blocks of scientific knowledge. An 'econological' rationale, mounted on the tripod of Ethics, Economics and Ecology, will explain and regulate the process by which nature is transformed into civilization.

'Econology' is the name that should be employed for the knowledge that will give a rationale to the set of norms that will explain and regulate the workings of what Maurice Strong has referred to as 'Ecodevelopment'.[6]

New ethics: new values

As is often the case, substitutes for decadent values are found in old values whose antiquity implies permanence rather than backwardness. The most ancient of these values, and for that very reason the most permanent, are those that emerged with the dawning of human consciousness. Our awareness of ourselves as individuals and as part of a specific social group, 'separate' from the rest of nature, goes hand-in-hand with our quest to set ourselves free from the bonds of nature – an accomplishment that has become our constant aim. Brandishing the arms of technological expertise, our every undertaking is pressed into the service of this quest for freedom. We sought to wage and win a war against a greater enemy: our annihilation by death. And, as the myths of eternity and youth proved to be beyond our grasp, we set about conquering free time by the might of our hands and brain.

There was a two-pronged quest for eternity: through dreams (gradually fulfilled) of increasing each individual's span of earthly life, and through the constant reduction of the time spent on the struggle to survive. The results were longer life expectancy and a greater amount of free time. Reduced work shifts, a shorter working week, annual holidays and leave – these all show how social organization was yoked to accomplishing this end.

In the 19th century, this social freedom grew to such an extent that it appeared potentially unlimited. More efficient social organization, however, fathered a contradictory rationale. Individualism and private ownership of the means of production, while boosting efficiency and productivity, generated three parallel, intrinsically associated phenomena.

First, the rationale that sought to increase free time was overwhelmed by the socio-economic system it created. Instead of extending free time, it multiplied output for consumption. Rather than fostering freedom, it fed the urge to consume, producing a teleological warp.

Secondly, for this rationale to work well and to allow technology to reduce the effort needed for survival, it was necessary for it to breed a certain social deformity. People were divided into two separate categories: those with greater freedom, who were doubly blessed by the conquest of free time and the upsurge in the level of consumption; and those with less freedom, forced to labour longer hours. The hardest hit by this deformity were those who, through lack of employment, were made absolute prisoners of the struggle for physical survival.

Thirdly, an ecological deformity was hatched. The drive for consumption took the shape of a riotous, unbridled process of transforming nature into goods and services, and so upset the ecological balance.

On the other hand, the possibility of attaining the terrestrial paradise Smith and other economists proposed hinged on the assumption that each individual, acting egoistically to maximize his or her own hedonistic enjoyment, would have the patience to wait for whatever length of time it took for all his or her peers' aspirations to be fulfilled. However, as Wanderley Guilherme dos Santos puts it, 'history revealed that the capitalist market would only work reasonably so long as the majority of the population did not act as egoistic maximizers. The relatively low level of social conflict, the prevalence of a notion of *public interest* overriding the personal interests of private individuals only persisted while the maximization of utilitarian ethics was not hegemonic. Once utilitarian ethics got the upper hand, the capitalist order became unstable, precarious, bankrupt.'[7]

Worse still, throughout this period (especially over the last two centuries) ethics has been trussed up in the logic of this process. Freedom has vanished as an ontological aspiration, its half-brother consumption taking its place. Technical advance, *per se*, has come to be seen as the mainspring of the historical process: the means by which we can assume the likeness of God. And in the process of this we either realize our fragility or utterly destroy ourselves.[8]

Formulating new ethical designs for the economic process entails coming up with a justification for technical progress. It would then be seen as a means rather than an end in itself. Throughout the last few centuries, the justification has been the need to raise the level of consumption – deemed to be a permanent, unquestionable and unlimited goal. The urge to consume, even when imposed and exploited by capitalists as a means of increasing capital, could be legitimized by an unconscious collective desire not merely to consume but to broaden the horizon of collective freedom. One could then portray this as society appropriating the fruits of nature and each consumer in turn appropriating the time expended by workers producing the goods and services that he or she consumes – time created by the power to transform nature into goods and services, transferred from workers to consumers through the latter's purchase power. Over-consumption, in turn, gives consumers the impression of possessing more available time and a longer lifespan.

Existential boredom with consumption, knowledge of its physical limits and the ethical crisis stirred up by unequal distribution among individuals – all these spark off a search for the root components of freedom. Consumer fatigue among those in a position to consume impresses upon them the fact that consumption cannot be an end in itself. The revolt among those who labour to produce but never manage to consume, when they eventually take stock of the drudgery to which they are enslaved (in view of the scant lifetime that they enjoy), points up the need to encounter some other end, a more permanent objective that was already underpinned by the very urge to consume. The ethical crisis completes the picture: we need a new framework.

In the 1960s circumstances arose that favoured contesting the present paradigm of civilization, and an awareness of the need to seek new motivations was consequently forged. There was a more mature awareness of the risk of a nuclear Armageddon. Direct observation of the effects of pollution and depredation on the environment abandoned the terrain of mere speculation, futurist imaginings or theoretical projections. The tedium of consumption reached absurd levels. Political conflicts (both in the domestic arena and as part of the process of decolonization) highlighted injustices. A crisis of conscience spread among scientists and technicians as they realized that they were not just the architects of utopias but also the masterminds of Frankensteins, sorcerers' apprentices and modern Pandoras. Finally the West began to view alternative concepts, religions and philosophies (especially those originating in the East) as a real possibility and not just as erudite curiosities.

The great ethical crisis of Western society looms large, and there are some signs that a broad-ranging ethical alternative is emerging. The common denominator is a constant rediscovery of the value of broadening the horizon of freedom – no longer synonymous with consumption but now manifested as the conquest of social free time, its even-handed distribution among individuals and its utilization by means of six components:

(1) The quest constantly to improve technological efficiency, so as to set people free from the bonds of material needs and promote prosperity, going hand-in-hand with the conquest of more free time.

(2) The quest for justice in the distribution of free time and of the fruits of prosperity among all members of society:

(3) The fostering of peace and respect for human rights to ensure that justice is not the preserve of particular nations, but spreads out in both directions: from each nation to the whole of humankind, and from each nation to every individual.

(4) The employment of free time and the fruits of prosperity in such a way that the transformation of nature and its by-products may raise the proportion of cultural goods defined by their human aspiration to beauty, truth and all forms of spirituality.

(5) A clear awareness that individual freedom and hedonism are a legitimate part of the drive to shape a civilizing project for the human race. Practices promoting them would then be viewed as a co-operative adventure in which all people are bound together – their individual traits being duly respected – in a collective movement that, far from imprisoning, sets the individual free.

(6) Finally, the solidarity of generations of the living with those that have passed, expressed through respect for the heritage handed down to them. At the same time, this heritage can be transformed and multiplied, thus conserving it for future generations. This permanent project for the human race can only be justified if we sally forth on our civilizing adventure with the utmost respect for the balance of the environment which nurtures and maintains life as a whole and the life of each species.

New Economics: the essentials

Awareness of the economic process first stems from observation of output at the level of each production unit. The term 'Economics' itself derives from the Greek concept of family output. As a field of knowledge, Economics is initially devoted to studying material production through the employment of natural resources and social relations. It also examines the way this production is distributed between the production agents. There was broad consensus on the tolerable moral limits to the size of a family production unit and to the amassing of personal and national fortunes. In his book *The Discoverers*, Daniel J. Boorstin quotes Aristotle's opinion that the wealth of a household or state should be limited. The limit was termed 'wealth'. Until the Middle Ages, there was general dislike for and disapproval of the accumulation of untold wealth.[9] The myth of Midas was the classic example of the inconvenience and the tolerable upper limit on the accumulation of worldly wealth.

As the centuries passed, the economic process evolved, attaining global scale through mercantilist expansion in the 16th century. The concept of wealth ceased to be an instrument of ethical limitation. The accumulation of personal and national fortunes not only became tolerable but was openly encouraged as a laudable goal. Midas ceased to be the object of ethical admonishment and became a shining example of entrepreneurial prowess. Over the last hundred years (and most noticeably over the last fifty), this process has acquired global dimensions. Economics, as a science, has begun to explain the mechanics of production and exchange on a planetary scale.

This new-found global scope, though, has been restricted to the geographical domain. Economics has been entirely unsuccessful in grasping the planetary dimension: its analyses have failed to account for the impact this process has had on the natural base that sustains it. Despite proving capable of progressing beyond the domestic focus Aristotle adopted in examining the phenomenon of production, modern economists have arrived at the end of the century wielding the same premises that have underpinned the theory of value since the 18th century, wholly ignoring the value of nature.

So long as production was limited and its effects slight enough to be readily absorbed by the environment, the theory of value had no need to take nature itself (viewed as a whole) into account. Resources were so slowly depleted that, given technical advances, they would never run out before substitutes could be found. The pace at which wastes were discharged was slow enough to allow for natural recycling and regeneration. However, now that the effects have become sufficiently serious to disturb the process itself, the essence of the economic process must needs be re-examined. It is essential that it should incorporate an ethical justification of the kind of product, the accumulation of wealth and the value of nature. Such an inclusion has not yet taken place.

Industrial Economics provides an excellent example. No industrialist gears his decision-making to consideration of the effects his industry may have on the ozone layer. Even the public sector, exclusively on the basis of economic theory, fails to take these effects into account. The reason is that, as a theory, Economics concentrates on people and their products and completely ignores nature. On the other hand, economic analysis is almost always short-term, its blinkers shutting out the long-term horizon. Besides, measurement of economic output has been confined to material production, with no consideration for a more permanent project of human liberation.

This state of affairs was engendered by a protracted process in which an explanatory ethic, initially framed by Adam Smith, gradually sank deep roots into the collective consciousness, eventually embodying the ethos of 'modern' society in all capitalist countries and even in those where 'real socialism' has been implemented this century.

The moment Economics attains global scale, the principles of its theory need to be modified. What is now happening to Economics is what happened to Physics fifty years ago. By boosting its impact to a planetary scale, through nuclear weapons, Physics discovered the need for regulatory ethics. The atom bomb saw to it that Physics became important for the population of the entire world. Economics has since followed suit. When it dawned on them that they had hatched a silent atom bomb in the shape of the modern industrial system, economists too felt the need for a new ethical yardstick – one which could not only explain but regulate as well.

Unlike physicists, who employ ethics to regulate science's power to manipulate minerals, plants and animals, economists will have to incorporate the new ethical principles into the very framework of their theory. The new ethics may well be utilitarian, but it is time for utilitarianism to be re-appraised and redefined, embodying new values, matching the following features that trace a broad outline of a new Economics:

(1) A new method for measuring economic output, capable of positing the conquest of freedom as the main objective of the human race. From

this angle, material production and consumption, however decisive, are just one aspect of the liberation process. The true purpose of the economic process will then be the increase and utilization of our global assets, especially in those nations where they are most concentrated. The material wealth vector will thus be an important component of these assets but no longer the sole, nor even the fundamental objective, which is now to be the sum of our cultural values.

The calculation of the net product generated by an economy should thus take particular account of its cultural wealth. Nature should be included in cultural wealth as a factor worthy of respect, the destruction of which should be deemed a loss when brought about by the economic process.

(2) The inclusion of the value of nature as a variable in economic analysis should relate to the sum total of life and to the efficient use of resources. Non-renewable resources, in particular, should not be depleted before they have become technologically obsolete through substitution by more efficient resources. Devastation of the environment, deforestation, the pollution of water-courses and the atmosphere should be recorded as losses in the reckoning of economic output.

(3) Long-term analysis constantly espousing a conservative approach to avoid running risks caused by over-optimism, which holds scientific and technological potential to be infinitely capable of solving each and every problem that crops up.

For this to be possible, the science of Economics must alter its bearings where the object of its criticism is concerned and undergo two substantial changes. Criticism, which has been levelled at methods and results, must now be concentrated on the basic premises and the objectives of the economic process. The first major break is the incorporation of ethical values. The evolution and consolidation of the science of Economics to date show the opposite to be the case: repeated attempts to imbue Economics with a neutral approach that would make it akin to natural sciences rather than an endeavour to submit it to the dictates of ethical norms. The second vital change lies in acquiring a global outlook that views the economic process as an integral part of natural and cultural transformations instead of singling it out from other social phenomena and examining only material transformations.

New Ecology: the global aspects

For a new economic theory to assimilate the global nature of the economic process in time and space, besides being equipped with ethical premises, the science of Economics will need a database at its disposal on which it can draw to gauge the global effects of each decision.

The only way to achieve this is for Economics to join forces with Ecology, a science that strives to understand the systemic relations involved in the entire web of life. If such an alliance is to prosper, though, the ecological outlook must equally be altered.

As a science, Ecology has become consolidated in recent decades due to the possibility of recording and analysing the entire set of activities nature sustains, by means of systemic, processable models. On the other hand, Ecology has been cast as the scientific foundation for an ethical commitment to nature conservation, opposing the absurd, destructive logic that the march of civilization has imposed over the past few hundred years. This commitment is legitimate. It is, however, inconsequential if it denies the primacy of the human race and its quest for freedom as the hub of the dynamics of nature itself.

What is required is not a conservationist slant seeking to supersede anthropocentrism but rather an outlook that can imbue anthropocentrism with the modesty of a species that acknowledges the limitations of its power, a species whose survival and civilizing enterprise depend on the natural base of Mother Earth. And a species capable of realizing that its drive to enhance civilization is an endeavour to expand a cultural heritage that directly depends on the existence and evolution of nature as a whole. The process by which nature is transformed by people will indeed be gripped by a nonsensical logic if it helps to undermine the heritage it aims to multiply. In this sense, the fight to conserve exhaustible natural resources is as vital as the campaign to prevent the extinction of economically relevant animal and plant species. For that matter, all natural species, even those with no productive value, should be preserved for the simple reason that, from the cultural point of view, they are part of our global heritage. Ecological respect thus obeys a logic ('econologic', if you will) that seeks to conserve resources and build up our heritage. This logic is grounded in ethics that continue to view the human race as the centre, but a reasoning centre now clad in the modesty of awareness of its limitations and objectives, conscious that nature is itself an asset.

Notes

1. There are, of course, exceptions in the history of science on both sides of the divide. The most noteworthy are Arnold Toynbee (especially in *A Study of History*, Oxford University Press, 1972, and *Mankind and Mother Earth*, Oxford University Press, 1976) and Darcy Ribeiro (in *The Civilizational Process*, Washington D.C., Smithsonian Institute Press, 1968, and *The Americas and Civilization*, New York, E.P. Dutton, 1972). Though moved by a very different concern, Teilhard de Chardin's *Le Phénomène Humain* (Paris, Editions du Soleil, 1955) is a landmark in examining the process of civilization in all its dimensions.

2. Serge Moscovici wrote a classic book on people's attitude to nature entitled *Essai sur l'Histoire de la Nature*, Paris, Flammarion, 1977.

3. An exception to this sort of attitude in the history of economic thought can be found in the work of the physiocrats. In analysing the value of products, Petty, Cantillon and Quesnay sought to include the cost of the land. Land, though, was deemed to be the property of the nobles, not of nature. As concepts, Nature and Land are not even mentioned in the subject indexes of the classic histories of economic thought, like J. Schumpeter's complete *History of Economic Analysis*, New York, Oxford University Press, 1954. *Economics in the Future: Towards a New Paradigm*, organized by Kurt Dopfer, London, Macmillan, 1976, to which six of the world's most important economists contributed, does not even touch on the subject.

4. Although the proposals tabled by the Club of Rome have been rejected for stressing the notion of zero levels, one should certainly not overlook its 1968 report, entitled 'The Limits to Growth', a milestone in international awareness regarding the risks of and bounds to the process of civilization.

5. Worldwide reaction to the death of the Brazilian rubber-tapper leader Chico Mendes in 1989 and *Time* magazine's choice of the Earth as 'man' of the year in 1988 are just two instances of this growing awareness. The size of the Eco-92 meeting in Rio de Janeiro is likewise a striking example of growing concern about this subject.

6. See the introduction to *Stratégies de l'écodéveloppement*, Paris, Les Éditions Ouvrières, 1980.

7. W. Guilherme dos Santos, *Poder, Propriedade, Ética*, mimeographed seminar on 'Ethics and Politics' held in Teresópolis (Rio de Janeiro State), 24-27 August 1989.

8. Fiction is often better than essays at conveying ideas. A short story by the Icelandic writer Erro Otrec, entitled 'The End of Afterwards' depicts this idea. See 'O Fim do Depois' in *Humanidades* Review, no. 20, Ano VI (1989), pp. 56-58. Brasília, University of Brasília Press.

9. See Daniel J. Boorstin, *The Discoverers: A History of Man's Search to Know His World and Himself*, Harmondsworth, Penguin Books, 1983, p. 652.

CHAPTER 3

The Underdeveloped Concept of Underdevelopment

The development of progress

The concept of progress is one of the most recent ideas to proceed from the collective imagination of the human race. It has only gained worldwide currency in the second half of the 20th century. Nevertheless, in this short time it has become so firmly ingrained that it is now difficult to imagine a time when history was not viewed as a continuous march towards industrial progress, where the future meant greater output.

Until recently, in what we label ancient cultures, time was always depicted as circular, quite unlike the linear trend needed to characterize progress. Yet economic theory, which emerged concomitantly with the idea of progress, has turned a blind eye to this alternative outlook.[1]

In a chapter on 'The Birth of History' in *The Discoverers*, Daniel J. Boorstin states:

> Hinduism was a religion of cycles. Later religions would be preoccupied with the Creation. They asked when, how and why the world first came into being, which led to speculation about the purpose of Creation and end of Man. But Hindus were more interested in Re-Creation. A modern view of history would require belief in unique, novel, world-reaching acts. While Hinduism has had many sacred documents, it has no one Sacred Text – no Bible that tells the one true story.
>
> The result was a wonderfully varied and constantly enriching Hindu jungle-garden of truth, but no path to the Truth. The Hindu lore of cycles carried the Hindu believer far beyond the round of the seasons, far beyond the rhythm of his own birth, life, and death, or that of his generation, into an unending universe of unending cycles, of cycles within cycles within cycles. The basic cycle, the kalpa, is 'a day in the life of Brahmâ', who was one of the three supreme Gods. Each kalpa lasts 4,320 million earthly years.[2]

The Aztec vision of time was even more clearly circular.[3] Progress could not be envisaged by such a concept of time.

As an expression of man's cultural improvement, the idea of progress is touched on by a select band of philosophers among the ancient Greeks: Hesiod, Protagoras of Abdera, Thucydides, and especially Plato. With a markedly different slant, the idea of progress can be observed in the Christian view of history as the spiritual ascent of the human race.[4] Indeed the Christian belief in a linear time was so widely accepted that Archbishop Usher officially declared 4004 BC as the year in which God created the world.[5]

In his *History of the Idea of Progress*,[6] Robert Nisbet states that:

> Ever since Hesiod, and even more so since Pythagoras, including Romans such as Lucretius and Seneca, Saint Augustine and his disciples, as well as the Puritans of the 17th century and later, and even the great prophets of progress in the 19th and 20th centuries, such as Saint-Simon, Comte, Hegel, Marx and Herbert Spencer, one finds an unwavering conviction that the very essence or nature of objective knowledge (science and technology) makes for progress, improvement, perfection.

But the idea of progress was still limited and held sway only among groups of thinkers striving to comprehend the world and piece together a rationale for it. Until the 19th century, the vast majority of the population in the Western world still clung to the rural sentiment that time was cyclical, reflected in the recurring seasons, feast-days and the constant renewal of life and death.

Not even among the 15th-century doctrinarians of the Reformation can one detect a hint of the idea of progress in its present sense of growing output. For Luther and all Protestants, work, frugality and abstinence were part of the personal sacrifice that would open the gates of Heaven, and were not intended to lay the foundations of material progress, as they inadvertently did. Only in the 18th century did thinkers of the Enlightenment and social philosophers begin to glimpse the possibility of progress in the current sense. But even then they were few in number and the idea had not yet penetrated social consciousness.

Progress continued to be a matter of advancement in the arts, sciences and in philosophical reflection, as the Greeks had proposed more than two thousand years earlier. Alternatively, it related to a state of spiritual bliss on earth and in heaven, as the Graeco-Judaic combination that fashioned the Christian concept of history in the West propounded, the sentiment of evolution being the mainspring of the entire process of civilization and its *raison d'être*.

Vico was perhaps the first thinker actually to strive to grasp the idea of progress in the modern sense. In an attempt to apply Francis Bacon's ideas about the natural world to history, in 1725 Vico published an essay whose title indicates just how receptive he was to the idea of progress: 'Principles of a new science on the connaturality of the nations, by means of which new principles of the natural law of peoples are also revealed.' But, as Edmund Wilson comments: 'Despite his originality, Vico never manages to make a clean break with the theological outlook which sets Heaven as the ultimate goal of improvement, salvation thus being an individual matter.'[7]

The idea remained vague and narrow in concept, cutting ice only with a handful of thinkers, having no place in the imagination and heart of the average man.

This made sense. Progress in its present sense could not have found a foothold outside the dynamic industrial system and would therefore not have been imagined by the corporate body of society. The lethargic pace at which civilization evolved in material terms prevented ordinary individuals, whose field of vision was circumscribed by their fleeting lifespan, from grasping the notion of progress. The plodding construction of Notre Dame cathedral down the centuries, or its permanent presence throughout each individual's lifetime, is less likely to convey the idea of progress than the rapid changes in urban space that came about at the end of the 19th century. Progress could thus only be grasped through painstaking intellectual analysis by select scholars of history.

Paradoxically, it is more the process of discarding the non-durable goods they produce than the permanence of the results of production that spreads and consolidates people's grasp of progress. Progress required the accumulation of capital, a technological base, and powers of social organization to become a widespread, generally held idea. These conditions made for growing efficiency that in turn increased the pace of output, enabling all to perceive progress in their lifetime.

The idea of progress only gains ground when the Industrial Revolution provides for the emergence and secures the historic continuance of the mercurial process of accumulation and technological advance. People only perceive progress by direct observation of the evolving economic process and by realizing the potential stored up in such a short span in industry – patently visible from the 19th century onwards and made all the more palpable in recent decades.

The linear view of time was to derive from slicker daily circulation of products manufactured and consumed on a wider scale. Agricultural society, tethered to the repetitive round of the seasons, hedged in by non-cumulative production, was indeed ill-equipped to conceive of accumulation or linearity. Next year's produce would be the same as this year's, the same quantity being entirely consumed in a cyclical passage of days and months whose rhythm was dictated by the changing (or unchanging) seasons. The oriental, circular notion of time is certainly not bred by ethnic factors (as certain racists might claim) nor by geographical circumstance; nor is it inspired by Buddha or Taoism. Rather, it springs from these societies' agricultural traits which are responsible for determining their cultural notion of time.

What is most surprising about the idea of progress is not its tender age but the speed with which it has lodged in our imaginations as an ingrained, intrinsic value. The idea has entered the collective consciousness of virtually all peoples, though some have rejected it on philosophical or religious grounds – as the hippies did in the 1960s, though in an ambiguous fashion. It is surprising how it has achieved supremacy over all other socially accepted ideas, to the extent that the remainder (happiness, peace, equality, freedom, justice, sovereignty), though they predate it, have come to be seen as offshoots of progress. The idea has come off the drawing-board and the printed page and out of the debating-chamber to occupy pride of place in all governments' plans and even in papal encyclicals as the *causa causans* of the human enterprise. As Nisbet says:

> Freedom, equality and popular sovereignty, each of these ideas has become not just something to be prized, something to be laboured for and expected; when placed in the context of the idea of progress, they could appear to be not only desirable but also historically necessary, their eventual accomplishment being inevitable. It was possible to demonstrate – as Turgot, Condorcet, Saint-Simon, Comte, Hegel, Marx, Spencer and many others actually did – that all history could be seen as a slow, gradual ascent, a continuous, necessary climb towards a determined end.[8]

There is a logic at work behind this overnight success. It is founded on the way in which the idea managed to combine Western desires –

the Christian image of heaven allied to the promise of a materialist utopia – while also glorifying the power of the human race.

In practice the feasibility of progress was demonstrated by the commercial integration that began to take shape in the twilight of the Middle Ages. It consisted of the eastward expansion of trade, the discovery of the Americas and the impact of capitalism with its machines, along with our desire to be the image of God and prove capable of building heaven on earth with our own hands. Together they made the appeal of progress even more irresistible.

The idea of progress possessed all the ingredients necessary to arouse the enthusiasm of Western thinkers, as one can ascertain from the progressive succession of ideas in Leibnitz, Locke, Vico, Adam Smith, Turgot, Condorcet, Hegel, Saint-Simon, Marx, Comte and Spencer. At the same time, the idea of progress was amply corroborated by reality (a rare historical phenomenon), gaining widespread public legitimacy as it was borne out by the turn of events; and so it permeated society's collective consciousness.

It was as if the idea of progress, and progress itself, were demonstrating, by the admission and evidence of their advantages, that progress did in fact exist. It became an irrefutable, universal truth. An idea that had descended from the Greeks as a synonym for cultural advancement was reformulated and enshrined as a concept specific to Economics and to those thinkers who, starting with Quesnay in the 18th century, were to be dubbed economists.

Economists became the proprietors of progress, but they also became prisoners of their perception of it. Proprietors because they distilled the idea of progress, reducing it to its material components. Prisoners because, in doing so, besides neglecting the other, higher values of humankind (now reckoned to be secondary or derivative), they now also began to believe in an irreversible trend of time and of the progress they had idealized.

Even when exceptions to the rule, like Malthus, voice their conviction about the limits to progress, they do so in isolation. Other economists, like Ricardo, simply raise doubts as to the viability of infinite material progress, but they go on to suggest ways of obviating the difficulties encountered and of reversing the tendency towards stagnation. Finally, a number of others, including Marx, perceive this limitation as a sign of contradictions at the core of the capitalist system. Their belief in progress, however, is just as unwavering, if not actually more steadfast, and leads them to propose social reforms as a means of resuming the trek along the path to infinite progress. The history of economic thinking has become the history of thought concerning the progress of the economy.

So the idea of progress arose, expanded and sent down roots, eventually being consolidated as a single, particular type of progress: economic progress. This can be reduced to Western modernity: constant raising of productivity and increased supply of economic goods made available to the entire population. In recent decades this specific concept has been further refined, to the extent that it is no longer a matter of growth but of unbridled growth in material output. Modern progress has completely lost touch with the Greek and medieval idea of cultural and spiritual advancement and has begun to be measured by the rate of growth of per capita output, only high and increasingly higher values of material production being deemed worthy of any degree of respect.

This specific concept becomes universally disseminated not merely on account of its theoretical propagating agents but, above all, because it takes concrete form in countries with wholly dissimilar characteristics. It is this feature that makes it the sole current universal concept of progress. All the members of societies actively strive to attain this sort of progress, concentrating their resources in the mimetic endeavour to repeat the success obtained by regions that have advanced farthest along this road.

Even cultural values are subject to a hierarchy established in line with the route progress maps out. All other ideas are then looked upon as disposable or held to be legitimate inasmuch as they chime in with the kernel idea – the achievement of progress. Aesthetic and ethical values and the notion of social efficiency are defined in terms of the contribution they may make to boosting the economy's gross product. Definitions of beauty, justice and sovereignty are subordinated to material progress. The very concept of culture is harnessed to this yoke that establishes the pecking order of superior or inferior cultures by the yardstick of their association with richer or poorer economies.

The idea of the common destiny of men, both in their material world and in the realm of the spirit, is tempered and moulded by the outlook of countries in the North. So much so that the idea of the North, instead of designating a geographical and navigational reference, has come to be associated with the correct direction for the social development of each country. To lose one's North is to lose one's bearings altogether – to stray from the highroad to progress, which is the only acceptable course. By way of contrast, the South is closely associated with backwardness.

The idea of progress has become so ubiquitous that, in Brazil, the term (and thus the concept) merits an inscription on the country's flag.* By explicitly enshrining the concept, Brazilian society committed its future to supine endorsement of the universal guidelines dictated by Europe, particularly those propounded by Comte. It was thus committed to standardized, Westernized modernization. No real choice was made; there was no prior survey of local circumstances, of the country's cultural values or natural resources and vocation. The nation was prevented from considering alternative goals, such as freedom and well-being, separately from consumption. As a result, they were dismissed as disorder and backwardness. Advocating such alternatives was out of the question, just as no one in their right mind would espouse damnation as a desirable alternative to salvation for the soul.

The speed at which the concept of progress gained general acceptance in human consciousness inevitably led to a search for instruments of social intervention that could help to hasten its accomplishment. Just as Christianity fathered crusades, missions and catechism, so the spontaneous cult of progress clamoured for its theology and acolytes. It took two hundred years from the moment Vico and others began to work out the idea of progress until the developmentalists took the stage.

The time lapse can be explained by the fact that the science of Economics, which claimed the idea of progress for its own, spent almost two centuries devoting itself to interpretating reality. Colonialist disdain for peripheral countries and belief in the natural trend of progress delayed the emergence of developmentalist techniques in economic thinking until very recently.

The need for fresh markets for large corporations, the consolidation of Economics as a science, and the evident signs of technological potential, all came to a head at the end of the Second World War, providing fertile ground for a burgeoning resolve to induce development across the world. A web of relations linking theorists and

---

* Translator's note: The Brazilian flag is inscribed with Auguste Comte's positivist motto 'Order and Progress'.

formulations, speculations and blueprints for development strategies immediately came into existence and set about defining the outline of a basic development theory, which now pervades the entire Third World.

The results were predictable and are now common knowledge: in two decades these countries advanced a century further than they would have done had natural evolution been left to its own devices. Wherever systematic policies were adopted, they proved capable of maintaining high rates of growth and of transforming the countries concerned, tailoring their realities to the indicators of progress. They all became industrialized, urbanized producers and even exporters of manufactured goods. Their societies began to display the outward signs of modernity. Transportation networks and energy grids were installed. And the machinery of state was modernized by authoritarian means. For approximately twenty years these countries experienced the euphoria of progress. This euphoria went under a variety of names and was hailed by a plethora of slogans, all of which reflected the miracle of the dream of instant progress come true.

The premature senility of the idea of progress

As fast as progress fanned out to the four corners of the Earth, in two fleeting decades it grew old before its time.

The success of progress in Western Europe and North America is as clear as its failure to deliver the promised utopia. At the end of the 1950s, the features that had legitimized progress – the combination of Greek ideals and Christian spirituality allied to the material well-being issuing from the Industrial Revolution – began to show signs of favouring consumption. Apart from Marxist criticism, and independent of it, Galbraith, philosophers of the Frankfurt School and others, working within the system and examining it from another angle, began to lay bare 'industrial consumer society'.[9] Their studies revealed and demonstrated its instability, its reliance on unproductive expenditure (especially the arms race), chronic unemployment and loss of basic cultural values. Such censuring of over-consumption, waste and bellicosity (the hallmarks of industrial society) was widespread in the late 1950s and early 1960s.

Just as progress took more than a century to permeate social consciousness, the first theoretical critique of progress took roughly a decade to become a collective conviction voiced by a whole sector of the population. Large groups of young people in rich countries realized that progress came at the expense of existential vacuity or even of their own lives on the battlefields. And, as they already possessed high consumption levels, they were in an ideal position to perceive that this central goal of modern civilization came at a price that was not worth paying.

As it had no coherent alternative proposal, the protest movement could hardly be expected to play a very consequential role. Besides, it was wholly unable to strike a chord with and spread to all the world's billions who had not had the benefit of reasonable levels of consumption. Moreover, the movement's militants were sitting ducks for accusations of living off the system they denounced. As a result, it soon petered out.

Despite the waning of the movement to counter consumption-based progress, the 1970s saw an upsurge in technical criticism of the same model of civilization that the hippies had decried in sentimental terms. This new onslaught was brought about by the demonstration, for the first time since Malthus, that unlimited growth was not viable in real terms on account of its relation to nature and not because of existential *ennui*.

Upon taking concrete form, progress revealed its impotence to build and deliver the utopia it promised. It fell short of human aspirations and failed to fulfil the human desire to be cast in God's image. It turned out to be a threat to the human race and a challenge to God, hounding us with regret and a painful sense of our own failure.

Generating previously unimaginable wealth for those who first glimpsed its results, progress demanded alienation and condemned millions to poverty, unemployment, and the iniquity of absurd professions and livelihoods. Worse still, it sponsored the irrational spectacle of unproductive labour, largely channelled into mass production of arms to fuel the wars required to keep the system operating.

Moreover, unrestrained output for feeding compulsive consumption led to the depletion of resources and environmental pollution, and so gradually posed a threat to the natural base that supports life itself. It also provoked dire mental distraction among large sectors of both urban and rural society, obsessed by the desire to sample what appeared to be the earthly paradise of consumption, at whatever social or ecological cost.

The significance of this stripping bare of hollow capitalist progress soon comes home to the developed countries, especially to the young who were born and have been brought up in an environment laden with the fruits of progress as a tangible reality rather than the stuff of dreams. They instantly sense how flawed the proposal is in terms of human fulfilment.

Criticism covered the entire spectrum from Sartre to Galbraith, McLuhan to the Club of Rome, from the hippies to the Red Brigades. Without refuting progress, it called its present practice into question across the board. For the first time since the anarchist cells of the 19th century, there was radical dissension quite distinct from Marx's rejection of capitalism.

Marx rejected capitalism for not being sufficiently progressive. To his mind, capitalism's main defect did not reside in progress but in its intrinsic limitation, which from a certain point would prevent the extension of progress due to under-consumption by the working classes. By paying workers less than the value of the product they manufacture, capitalists retain part of production for investment in new undertakings. These rarely see the light of day because the working classes, too poor to purchase the goods they produce, generate a slump in demand that prevents progress. The Marxist proposal consisted in implementing socialism so that, by distributing the entire value of production among workers, productive forces could grow in an unfettered, planned manner that would avert crises. Permanent progress would then be achieved. Marx was thus an obdurate champion of progress who hammered capitalism because the system was incapable of promoting it to the full.

There can be no doubt that Marx made a major contribution to human thinking by explaining the absurd logic underpinning capitalism. Yet, more than any other thinker, Marx remained faithful to the idea of progress and was the greatest exponent and prophet of unlimited human progress. In this sense, despite his radical political opposition to the ruling classes of his day, he was actually a well-behaved critic within the philosophical tradition that originated in Greece, traversed the Middle Ages, blended with Christianity in the Renaissance and through the Reformation, becoming consolidated during the Enlightenment, and persisted in all subsequent optimistic views that descend from this line of Western thought.

Keynes believed the solution to the dilemma posed by Marx consisted in the state intervening to buy up, directly or indirectly, all the surplus output that workers prove incapable of purchasing. Unlike Marx, who argued for the abolition of capitalism, Keynes endeavoured to find a way of preserving the political interests of capitalists.

Neither Marx nor Keynes rejected the idea of progress. On the one hand, Keynesian Economics sought to revive the forward march of progress within capitalism; on the other hand, Marx's socialist alternative was likewise keen to foster progress once the technical contradictions that thwarted its advance had been resolved. The revival Keynes devised has been under siege for some time now with the encroachment of inflation, rising government debt and diminishing growth rates and inefficiency of the state and welfare system. The socialist alternative has come under severe pressure from political dissatisfaction, the inefficiency of global planning when it comes to dealing with day-to-day problems, and, above all, from frustration at the failure to satisfy the desire of the masses to consume.

Trapped in this dilemma, unable to measure up to expectations and prevented from advancing, progress, as we have known it over the last two centuries and especially in recent decades, has reached breaking point in the countries where it originated and attained its peak. The end of the socialist experience killed the alternative possibility of an industrial civilization beyond capitalism. The ecological crisis menaces the ideological basis of progress and the economic system.

Importing the idea of progress into the South

The idea of progress, like all other social concepts that have currently gained universal scope, was bred in the Northern hemisphere. It was a dialectic process that moulded an ideology made legitimate by its efficiency in transforming the world and by its ability to forge ethical acceptance of the results obtained.

These ideas have arrived ready-made and pre-packaged in the countries of Latin America, Asia and Africa. They have not germinated on home ground, nor have they been legitimized by social observation of their results or by the collective consciousness of the local population. They have been foisted on these countries by the imperative of international integration, by the expanding activities of multinational corporations since the beginning of the 20th century, and particularly during recent decades. Ever since the 'discovery' of

Brazil in 1500, foreign companies had always existed and operated as if in an enclave, exerting almost no influence on the local population which was made up of slaves and foreigners committed to the interests of the metropolises from which they hailed. If it existed at all at that stage, the idea of progress applied to the metropolitan nations, not to the colonies in which their investments were situated.

When progress (previously conceptually elaborated in rich countries) set foot in newly independent countries during the course of the 20th century, it proved poorly suited to their cultural and natural environment and ill matched to the needs of the local population. The industrial system installed, the urban culture and consumer standards imposed, the levies raised in the form of capital and natural resources – all were dictated by standards established in Europe and North America after centuries of evolution.

Despite this, progress sported an instant sheen and met with no resistance. Development measures and policies obtained nationwide consensus for the first time ever in the history of these countries. Right across the political spectrum everyone rallied round the objectives and the principal means employed to implement them, even when both sides levelled fierce criticism at the method of bestowing bounty and sharing out the benefits between foreign business concerns and national companies on the one hand, and between capital and labour on the other.

The elation with which this imported model was greeted and the exultation at its potential to transform enabled the idea of progress to gain instant admittance to the minds of the local élites. Conservative criticism came from a handful of politicians and economists who either feared industrialization and urbanization, anxious lest local power should slip from their clutches, or else upheld an outmoded belief that free international trade was the best means of maximizing returns that they deemed to be on a par with those of progress. These groups were out on a limb, however, and their voice amounted to little more than nostalgic bleating at the passing of an age that was fast ebbing before the eyes of those dazzled by the brash glitter of progress.

In the progressive camp, criticism was confined to two points: internal distribution of the proceeds; and economic dependence, which indicated that the international distribution of the benefits would be frankly unfavourable to developing countries. The dependency theory critics explained the backwardness of some countries through the dependent relations they had with developed countries. They singled out economic backwardness as the root cause of poverty, believing it to be the offspring of the distorted international distribution of labour which saddled countries with either essentially agricultural or essentially industrial profiles. Moreover this distortion was further aggravated by the downward trend in relative prices of the primary products on which poor countries depended for their income. These products persistently performed badly in relation to the prices of the manufactured goods poor countries were obliged to import. On these grounds, dependency theorists defended the protection of national industry as a means of offsetting dependence and restoring a just distribution of value through a new international organization of labour.

These dependency theorists maintained industrial development, along the lines of that implemented in developed countries, as the prime objective. They were against the country's economic dependence but adopted a dependent stance in defining the objectives of the independent economy they propounded. They wanted to substitute imports but in fact they imported the idea of substitution.

In criticizing the dependent economic model, they fell prey to cultural dependence so insidious that they failed to notice it. They denounced poor countries' economic exploitation as the source of backwardness in Third World societies but were blind to the fact that the definition of progress (and so also of backwardness) employed in their analysis was formulated on the basis of the cultural dependence to which they themselves were prone. They lambasted economic dependence using an imported ideological framework as a whip, unwittingly failing to realise that they were equally flailed by its lashes. This was the predictable effect of the upbringing of an élite groomed to the standards of the metropolitan countries where they pursued their studies and from which they drew inspiration.

Though they carped about the fact that poor countries could not hold the tiller of their destiny (since they were subjected to the rules of domination of international economic relations), the dependency theorists did not scrutinize their own theories which blatantly prevented poor countries from themselves defining the objectives of their destiny. They elaborated development plans with strategies aimed at delivering independence that would allow them to go their own way, free from external domination. Meanwhile, however, they unquestioningly accepted that these strategies should be geared to meeting targets pre-set by the very countries whose domination they shunned. They espoused economic autonomy for backward countries to achieve progress but had no concern for an autonomous definition of the objectives of progress.

The idea of progress was thus automatically imported on account of the dependency theorists' cultural dependence.

On importing the concept of progress, the populations of the Third World discovered and again imported the concept of underdevelopment. They applied it to themselves by using the developed world as a comparative yardstick.

Each poor country thus became underdeveloped the moment it imported the idea of development without analysing it, contesting it, adapting it or making it match indigenous values and resources. In order to classify itself as underdeveloped, it underdevelopedly imported the concept of underdevelopment. In order to formulate the idea of dependence, the dependency theorists likewise bowed down to cultural dependence.

This meant that for the first time in history the thinking élites of a people acquiesced in being labelled 'barbarous'. In its etymological Greek and Latin origin, the word was used as a synonym for foreign or alien, expressing cultural difference, distrust, curiosity, mockery and even envy, but never conveying a sense of inferiority with the attendant disparagement of the other's culture. The concept and sentiment of underdevelopment that poor countries subscribed to and applied to themselves, tailored to imported standards of consumption and patterns of behaviour, imposed on their own people submission to foreign, barbarous influence.

This ideological option was not divorced from reality. These theorists carved out their ideas in an environment fraught with real poverty where the essential values of civilization were concerned. They took a long, hard look at low education and health standards, dismal productivity that allowed no free time for cultural activities, and severe undernourishment. In this sense, the idea of development and the dependency theory represent a milestone in the attempt to examine and influence the transformation of society. But its theorists then confined themselves to explaining the absence of all the essential values as a direct consequence of economic backwardness. They construed their countries' economic objectives as identical to those of other countries. In so doing, they overlooked the costs and limitations that would ensue and disdained many of their own societies' essential values, writing them off as undesirable, for they would have to be crushed and swept aside by the bulldozer of development.

Once each country had accepted its underdeveloped condition, all its efforts were concentrated in the drive to mimic the objectives of countries reckoned to be developed. After importing ideas of progress and backwardness, development and underdevelopment, they went on to import the definition of essential values, necessities and means. The entire *modus operandi* of society was duly adjusted and its natural resources pressed into the service of attaining these objectives.

The strategy elected for promoting growth was industrialization based on the substitution of imports that were not yet being made or were made to order for a small minority identified with consumer standards in rich countries.

Demands were imported so that the Third World could cease importing the goods that satisfied them. Substitution was imported. Nationalism was used so that the goods required for satisfying the demand that had been subserviently imported could be produced locally.

Instead of their socio-economic systems being geared to their real needs – identified by biological and cultural criteria – and tailored to their available economic, cultural and natural resources, these societies chose *a priori* to implement wholesale the economic structure they desired (based on the so-called developed model) and believed to be the by-product of progress.

In their anxiety to attain progress through the importation of needs and means for implementing the rich nations' model of development, underdeveloped countries ran deeply into debt, raped their cultures, depleted their resources, concentrated income and wealth, resorted to authoritarian régimes and segregated their societies. Given the deep differences in income, in needs, in culture, in the availability of financial and natural resources and of techniques, the process of development could only be sustained by a further round of concentration of wealth, authoritarianism, depletion of natural resources, and raping of local culture.

Although there are no ideologically neutral technical standards for arguing against one or other type of social evolution, one can rightly assume that each model involves costs capable of maiming the strategy adopted.

The financial crisis that has driven many states to bankruptcy, the economic crisis that has drastically reduced the level of growth, the social crisis that has provoked increasing impoverishment after five decades of growth, the political crisis that has fostered discontent and growing instability, the ecological crisis hastened by extensive burning and rapid environmental degradation, all indicate that the civilizational model being implemented in most Third World countries, especially in countries like Brazil, is seriously at risk. These countries would appear to have reached a turning point involving the exhaustion of the model of progress hitherto adopted and the emergence of a question as to what new alternative can be chosen.

The progress of the idea of progress

In this fundamental struggle to broaden the horizon of freedom, we will not be able to escape our vocation for seeking to understand and mould our destiny, through changing the concept of progress.

The options before us range from the most radical denials of the prevailing system, along the lines of the hippy revolution or the Chinese revolution prior to the recent reforms, to an inexorable plodding along the course set by the Industrial Revolution in the West.

To all appearances, these positions point in opposite directions, confirming or denying outright the prevailing concept of progress. Wholly denying such progress is absurd, for it has been a constant presence over the last two hundred years and, despite all the dissatisfaction that has risen, it holds out as an entrenched human aspiration. Release from the struggle for survival, either by setting one's sights on the technological future or by casting one's mind back to a past paradise, is a human aspiration as popular as freedom, justice, peace or love. On the other hand, our present stage in the struggle for and attainment of progress clearly demonstrates its drawbacks and unfeasibility.

Having acknowledged these two points, the alternative is to formulate a new concept that will reinvent progress, incorporating ethical values and a real sentiment of progress into the idea of progress. Being developed should mean being open to the idea of society that each people strives to achieve.

Among the essential values to be incorporated is the basic premise that progress should be governed by the venture of constantly rolling back the horizon of freedom for the individual and for each nation. This concept of freedom should include an efficient and balanced appropriation of nature so that future generations can make use of it; the availability of free time for practising cultural activities; national sovereignty; justice and peace. It should also be flexible enough to respect such definitions and combinations as each society considers best suited to its cultural purposes and natural resources.

The first step towards promoting development must be an independently obtained definition of development. It must be based on progress that upholds the essential feature of subordinating the economic process to values and objectives that reach well beyond straightforward economic targets. To achieve this, it is vital to vanquish the myths created by the primacy of the viewpoint of Economics which is shackled to archaic premises.

Notes

1. Despite the vast scientific, philosophical and theological bibliography on the subject, perhaps no other work has managed to portray the idea of circles of civilization, as opposed to continual progress, as well as a science-fiction story by Isaac Asimov entitled 'Nightfall'.

2. Daniel J. Boorstin, *The Discoverers: A History of Man's Search to Know His World and Himself*, Harmondsworth, Penguin Books, 1983, p. 558.

3. See Tzvetan Todorov, *La Conquête de l'Amerique: La question de l'autre*, Éditions du Seuil, Paris, 1982.

4. This idea is very well protrayed in another science fiction story: Arthur C. Clarke's 'The End of Childhood'.

5. In the modern era, Physics has extended this concept of linearity even further and in a more materialist manner, calculating the beginning of time itself. But in taking this great leap, Physics has opened the way for a resumption of the idea of cycles for, if time had a starting point, that suggests there could have been another time before it. It is not just a matter of chance that the last twenty years have seen the budding of attempts to blend Western rationality and linearity with the circular vision of the East. One book in particular raises such considerations: Fritjof Capra's *The Tao of Physics*, New York, Bantam Books, 1976.

6. Robert Nisbet, *History of the Idea of Progress*, Basic Books, 1980.

7. Edmund Wilson, *To the Finland Station*.

8. Nisbet, *op. cit.* p. 181.

9. John Kenneth Galbraith, *The New Industrial State*, New York, Signet Books, 1967.

CHAPTER 4

Modernizing Modernity

The bomb that liberates

The awesome effects of the two atom bombs detonated in August 1945 sowed deep doubt in the public mind about the role of science as an instrument for human advancement. When it reached the paradoxical point of jeopardizing existence, human knowledge began to devise means for controlling the use to which its brainchildren were put.

Our collective awareness of the risks involved in high-tech war led us to realize the need for international peace. Atomic power highlighted the pressing need for disarmament.

As was the case with the atom bomb in the field of Physics, awareness of the threat posed by the productivity bomb has been instrumental in creating the need for us to resolve the paradox that we menace the very existence of civilization by our endeavour to carry through our civilizational enterprise. Yet the perverse effects of the economic productivity bomb have not yet been sufficient to cancel out the contribution economic growth has made to the building of a potentially freer society.

Throughout history, human society has marched towards the conquest of freedom. Thanks to progress, we have almost entirely overcome our reliance on hostile nature; we have substantially reduced the number of work hours required for physical survival; and we have used the resulting free time in the production of cultural goods and in our quest for beauty and truth.

Our present plight consists in our possession of tremendous powers to achieve our objectives coupled with the risk of total destruction of our project for advancing civilization. One cannot fail to notice that the power of knowledge, though the fruit of an historic, concerted effort, is not evenly distributed – and this in turn highlights the injustice of the even distribution of the noxious effects of this power. Science has not extended the benefits of Nuclear Physics to all (through energy generation or applications in Medicine), but the dreaded consequences of nuclear accidents, such as the leakage of radioactive material at Chernobyl or the breaking open of an abandoned caesium capsule in central Brazil, are visited indiscriminately on all in the vicinity.

To awareness of both the potential and the risks is added a sense of injustice, preparing the terrain for an ethical revolution entrusted with regulating the use of the scientific and technological revolution.

The time is ripe for us to implement the ideological revolution that is needed if we are to shake off the fetters of the senseless logic that has prevailed in recent decades. This is most apparent in countries like Brazil which possess sufficient natural resources to build an increasingly efficient society unhampered by material shortages. Wanton destruction is sufficiently advanced in Brazil to raise consciousness of the need for the responsible use of nature. The country has a sophisticated scientific, technological and economic infrastructure but there is clear discontent at the results obtained. There is, in particular, great discontent at the social distribution of these results. Most other countries are either too poor in natural resources and infrastructure or else too rich and bound by commitments to their production systems and development models, besides being untroubled by the same pitch of crisis and discontent.

In the political sphere, a degree of maturity has been attained that will, over the coming years, demand a development model bred by a new rationale. The need for this is already beginning to be recognised. Part of Brazil's population is already starting to contest the developmentalist ideology that has guided and goaded the country for almost half a century.

The next step is to formulate ethical objectives and outline a new model of well-being, sloughing off the blinkered approach that was bent on achieving higher consumption alone. Instead, one should make allowance for an increase in global wealth and strive to introduce a new economic rationale that will turn the 'other bomb' into a bomb that liberates instead of destroying. The world as a whole can similarly be viewed from this angle.

Exorcising modernity

From the moment the idea of progress permeated the consciousness of the human race and Economics made the notion of modernity its preserve, a generally-accepted fetish was placed upon a pedestal. According to its dictates, all people required a single destiny, a destiny measured by strict, inflexible standards determined by the technical advances utilized in the production system.

Modernity – taken as a synonym for the future one desires – was defined by the techniques to be used. An economic rationale was then concocted to justify the use of such techniques. Objectives related to the essence of the human condition were thus made subordinate to the accomplishment of the purposes sought by the economic rationale. Ethical values had to be relinquished to bring about this state of affairs.

This fetish urgently needs to be exorcised, and the concept of what 'modern' means needs to be redefined on the basis of goals consistent with the objectives of a permanent civilizing process. Ethical values must define the social objectives to be striven for; the economic rationale must serve these objectives; and techniques must be the result of this rationale, not a determining variable.

Brazil is an example of the effects of this fetish and of the possibilities of reversing it.

The ethical purpose

Three technological factors, already well established in Europe at the end of the 15th century, made Brazil a going concern as a country: the knowledge and instruments required for navigating long distances, the technology for building large sea-going vessels, and the techniques for producing sugar. Other associated factors included the abundant, highly productive land available in the new country for obtaining this product, and colonial, political and economic relations. All this meant that Brazil's future as a nation was from the outset subordinated to the international economy.

Unlike European society, where the economy was part and parcel of the concept of nationhood (its nobility, art, sovereignties, etc.), in the new country economic activity was an adjunct of the 'European' world.

Five hundred years of history* have done nothing but confirm this initial situation. From product to product, from sphere of influence to sphere of influence, by the extermination of the indigenous population and laying waste the environment, everything has obeyed the same logic to the last letter.

---

* Translator's note: Brazil was 'discovered' by the Portuguese in 1500 AD.

More recently, the outward form has changed with the switch to industrialization, but the rationale and the central objectives that have steered the country on its course have remained the same. The installation of infrastructure, the destruction of the environment, the education and health systems, culture – all those square with the concept established centuries ago.

Today there is growing dissatisfaction with the results that this scheme has produced. It stems from the degradation of life which manifests itself on seven fronts:

(1) Social degradation, which foists a species of apartheid on the country which is then divided off into two separate social groups. This clearly impedes the constitution of a nation and makes life unbearable for both sides: one suffering the violence of misery on the doorstep of wealth; the other suffering from the threat to its wealth posed by encroaching misery; both exposed to the risk of brutal violence.

(2) Environmental degradation that underscores the impracticability of a country bent on the desertification of its forests, the poisoning of its water courses, the pollution of its atmosphere, and the rampant depredation of its natural resources.

(3) Degradation of the country's foreign relations, as the result of a model based on an economy dependent upon foreign technology, foreign capital and foreign natural resources, an economic strategy demanding growing indebtedness, which clearly indicates submission to the arbitrary practices and exploitation of the international finance system.

(4) Cultural degradation of its largely uneducated population as well as of an élite that is loath to commit itself to the country's interests and real needs, preferring to conjure up a socio-economic framework divorced from the country's cultural values and unsuited to its natural environment.

(5) Political degradation that breeds grave social instability in the shape of debt, maladjustments and all sorts of imbalances, of which monetary inflation is but one instance. As a consequence, acute individual moral degradation stemming from an atmosphere of social perversion, loss of confidence in oneself and in national institutions, fear of the future, and a total lack of solidarity concerning the nation's values and global interests.

(6) Degradation of the machinery of state which, after efficiently serving the purposes of organization and repression in prompting an élitist, dependent scheme, then founders in financial, political and administrative terms.

(7) Realisation, for the first time, that it is not necessarily the country with the brilliant future it once thought it was, but a country with a dark, deformed, debilitated future, despite all its immense potential and available resources. National awareness gradually takes heed of imperfections lodged in the fallacious logic of the nation's enterprise and begins to realize how inconsequential are the objectives it has pursued for five centuries. It registers the fact that output has grown, that the country has a self-sufficient production system supplying the market with home-grown products, that it possesses a considerable surplus for export, has become one of the economic powers of the Western world, and has installed an appreciable economic and scientific-technological infrastructure, but remains just as poor, dependent, uneducated and lacking in health as before, and continues to depredate its own resources. It realizes that these advances are false and that the indicators of its performance over the last fifty years have failed to depict the full extent of the nation's drama because they reflect partial objectives.

From the social and economic point of view, Brazil provides a condensed portrait of the entire planet. According to all purely economic indicators – GDP, industrial output, the level and make-up of its exports – the country has succeeded in making the change from a backward to a 'modern' economy. A broader assessment of this evolution from the perspective of civilization, not restricted merely to economic measurement, shows that, as a nation, Brazil has made no great progress this century. In some respects, it has actually been back-pedalling. Its global assets may even have shrunk. This is further aggravated if one considers the future consequences and side-effects of a divided, uneducated society, wasting what remains of its cultural heritage and global assets.

In order to reverse this trend we must redefine national priorities and objectives by injecting an ethical ingredient that enables the population to live in harmony with itself, with other nations and with nature. This must be:

(1) A society that will not countenance the misery of under-nourishment, poor health, or lack of basic education, housing, leisure and other social services and consumer goods for meeting its needs; a society in which the individual does not feel that his or her personal stability is jeopardized by the state's instability; one that is capable of constantly raising the productivity of labour.

(2) A society that uses the free time conquered by economic productivity to expand cultural activities of all kinds, including religious worship and political militancy.

(3) A society that distributes the benefits of consumption and cultural activity among its population in an increasingly even-handed manner so that they can enjoy equal measures of free time and individual freedom for such ends.

(4) A society that does not posit stability as a by-product of social equilibrium but acknowledges its link with ecology in maintaining a lasting balance that will ensure efficiency for future generations.

(5) A society that is aware of itself and ascribes priority to increasing its specific heritage and assets but at the same time realizes that it is just a small portion of humankind in a fast-moving trend towards interdependence and integration.

The first step to be taken in measuring up to the new purposes of Economics is to review the definition of national problems. In recent decades, Brazil's politicians, on the right and left, have played the part of economists' messenger-boys and spokesmen. The general public itself has begun to make myths of economic problems, identifying them as the country's most serious challenge. The country's image of itself is culled from its economic programmes; worse still, its long-term national aim is wholly identified with circumstantial measures designed to deal with short-term difficulties.

If we are to redefine national objectives we must subordinate the economy to a global project. We must define the country's real problems: absence of a collective national consciousness, illiteracy and foundering basic education, infant mortality and lack of medical assistance, malnutrition, social instability, dependence, the pervasive atmosphere of violence, the housing crisis, want of leisure, low productivity, depletion of the nation's natural and cultural assets, and a host of other major problems that must be tackled and solved to make the country truly modernized. The economy must be viewed as a means of attaining social objectives; the problems peculiar to the economic process must be considered difficulties and obstacles to be overcome in the drive to accomplish these objectives. Measurements of the annual performance of society and the economy must take stock of the costs of despoliation of nature, infant mortality, loss of sovereignty, and so on.

Bringing the economy to heel

By the year 2000, a sizeable portion of the population of today's greatest world superpower will be semi-illiterate. Expressing its concern with dwindling future sales that depend on the level of literacy, the USA's publishing industry estimates that: 'By the year 2000, two in every three North Americans may be illiterate. Today, 75 million adults, about one in every three North Americans, cannot read properly.'

Meanwhile, in a small, poor country like Cuba, almost 100% of the population is literate and all schoolchildren complete secondary education. In terms of health standards and medical assistance, the situation is much the same.

The reason for this is the philosophical approach to social problems. The prevailing American ethos holds that social concerns must bow down to economic expediency: if the economy were dynamic, society would inevitably possess the kind of social assistance it requires. Cuba, of course, has adopted the opposite stance: it has made economic interests subordinate to social designs. Western European countries, meanwhile, have sought to dovetail the encouragement of consumption with the fulfilment of social needs.

Brazil is an extreme case of dogged application of the North American strategy. The country has totally neglected social objectives in order to promote a systematic policy of economic growth. There has been tacit assurance that economic progress will automatically usher in a higher level of welfare and an overall improvement in sanitary conditions, health, education and culture. There has been a concerted drive to expand investments in economic infrastructure. Even strategies in social sectors have been adapted to achieving this overriding economic goal. Public health services and housing programmes have been viewed as means of enhancing the dynamics of the productive sector rather than as ends in themselves.

The consequences of this policy are plainly visible in economic and social indicators. Between 1900 and 1987 there were only eight years in which Brazil's Gross Domestic Product recorded negative growth; for nearly half the period, the rate has been over 5%; in fourteen years, a staggering annual growth rate of over 10% has been recorded.[1]

In its first hundred years as a Republic, Brazil has been transformed from a rural society into a country where 70% of the population live in urban areas, including some of the world's largest cities.* The country's economy had previously revolved around its exports of three cash crops. In a short space of time, Brazil built up a vigorous industrial economy that has catapulted it into the ranks of the world's ten biggest economies in terms of gross product. It is virtually self-sufficient in all branches of industry, and its manufactures (ranging from textiles to aircraft and including an automobile industry capable of manufacturing a million cars a year) have proved competitive on the international market. The chemicals sector, likewise, manages to supply most of Brazil's domestic demand.

Brazil is linked length and breadth by a formidable communications network that includes modern inter-state highways and a high quality telecommunications system with country-wide television broadcasting and telephone networks. Brazil's scientific, technological and higher education infrastructure places it in a position to debate with the rest of the world on an equal footing, though it is still at a relative disadvantage in quantitative terms. The country's technological prowess and administrative competence have enabled it to build the world's largest hydroelectric power plant, install a nationwide electric energy grid and compete keenly on the international market in this sector. It has set up an innovative, extensive system of substituting alcohol for oil as a fuel while also building a sophisticated, autonomous oil industry that efficiently masters all the techniques from prospecting and drilling to petrochemical production, and has even set a series of world records in deep sea exploration. Brazil possesses some of the world's most renowned surgeons and has hospitals capable of providing top quality services that include airborne ambulances and state-of-the-art intensive care units.

---

* Translator's note: Brazil became a Republic in 1889.

Thus, as we near the end of this century, Brazil can boast indicators that are the very definition of modernity. Despite this, it is plagued by a frightening social predicament and will enter the 21st century beset by a very real risk of domestic and external financial collapse, as well as of social chaos and turmoil.

While Brazil strode towards becoming a major economic power, all its welfare standards (especially in health and education) were plummeting as a direct consequence of the fact that economic interests prevailed over social concerns. The only services that consistently improved were those which, besides being required for installing the country's economic infrastructure, were also the means of boosting the dynamics of the industrial sector, such as telecommunications and the inter-state and urban transport system.

Subsidies and favourable exchange and credit policies have made Brazil one of the world's biggest exporters of agricultural produce. Its agriculture is highly mechanized and well supported in technical terms, both in the commercial sphere (Brazil is linked to all the major international exchanges and commodities markets) and in terms of scientific back-up (Brazil has some of the world's most competent scientists in this field).

Between 1970 and 1985 production of cash crops for export grew at rates of over 100%, reaching as much as 359% in orange production and an astounding 1,112% in soybean production. Sugar-cane cultivation was increased to meet the new demand for fuel alcohol to substitute for oil imports and keep the local automobile industry afloat. Meanwhile, production of crops for domestic consumption shrank, or else grew slower than the birth rate. Only two crops grown for the domestic market saw increases that topped population growth because they either substituted imports or were partly exported. As a result, the incidence of malnutrition and ailments associated with the lack of a balanced diet increased dramatically.

Today, 120 million Brazilians live in poverty, 53 million of them eking out an existence below the breadline, while 20 million of these paupers vegetate in absolute wretchedness. This makes Brazil the second largest pocket of misery on the planet. No less than 25 million of Brazil's poor are children wholly abandoned to their own devices or living in sub-human conditions due to their families' indigence. Roughly 70 million Brazilians suffer varying degrees of under-nourishment, 30 million of whom have reached such a dire state of malnutrition as to be diagnosed as suffering from endemic famine. Even in a rich state like São Paulo, a quarter of the infant population is under-nourished.

In addition to this serious state of under-nourishment, Brazil's population is afflicted by a host of primitive diseases. Whole segments of the population are infected with leprosy, dengue, tuberculosis, Chagas disease, malaria, cholera, etc. The average life expectancy for the entire country, irrespective of social class, is 63 years; in the poverty-stricken North-east it drops to less than 50 years, and among low-income families it is barely better than the baneful toll which was the scourge of European societies in the Middle Ages.

Average infant mortality before the age of one year is 87 in every 1,000 live-born children. But this overall rate does not reflect the fact that in some family income brackets mortality is almost 200 in 1,000. Of those who survive, 240 will enter the next century without learning to read or even write their own names. Only nine in every 100 will complete secondary school; a mere two will enter higher education and less than one, on average, will actually graduate from university with a satisfactory degree.

It is not just the progress of society that is retarded; the economy built up in Brazil is beginning to show clear signs of fragility. Brazil's external debt obliges the country to expend 5% of its Gross Product on interest payments alone. This is tantamount to donating the labour of twice the number of slaves that existed in Brazil a hundred years ago, when slavery was abolished.

On the ecological front, Brazil has brutally despoiled its territory, fouling its water courses, atmosphere and beaches, and, more seriously, felling and devastating its forests: only 3% of the Atlantic Forest in the coastal strip survives, and some experts estimate encroachment on the Amazon Forest to be advancing at a rate of 0.7% of the total area every year.

Economically-consolidated, modern Brazil thus sits uneasily with poor, primitive Brazil, making up a picture of a fragile country bereft of an ethical backbone for framing its nationhood.

The fact of the matter is that Brazil is perhaps the most segregated of modern societies, including even South Africa. In today's Brazil, and increasingly so as time passes, there are schools for the rich and no schooling for the poor; shopping centres to which the poor are only admitted to carry out the most menial tasks; fenced-off streets and condominiums where only residents have right of way; clinics and spas for rejuvenating the rich and bleak hospital corridors where the poor are dumped to die. Even the currency – a refinement never dreamt of in South Africa – is separate, segregating those who can protect themselves from searing inflation from those whose earnings are insufficient to give them access to monetarily updated funds and are thus obliged to carry a grubby currency reserved for the have-not masses.

Brazil's predicament is wholly different from the famine of countries blighted by the strife of civil war or of regions where prolonged drought has provoked food shortages. As the social scientist Hélio Jaguaribe puts it: 'Brazil's accomplishment is minute when compared to what other countries with regimes as diverse as Cuba, Colombia, Chile and Jamaica have achieved. There is a flagrant incongruity between the modest gains obtained in terms of welfare and the huge surge in economic growth in the seventies.'[2] Famine in Brazil is the result of the priority given to the economy and to economic growth. An excessively keen appetite for economic growth has brought widespread hunger. Poor health, anaemia, intestinal parasitic ailments and a high drop-out rate among Brazilian schoolchildren struggling to make the grade have ensued.

The only solution is to change the way the social process is viewed in Brazil and the Third World, bringing economic interests to heel instead of subjugating social concerns to the economic imperative.

Some economists who are critical of Brazil's economic growth model insist that this is a problem of income distribution. They propose a general wage rise in the belief that this would instantly boost agricultural production for the domestic market. The correlation is unfortunately not that obvious, and it is defended on the basis of the same economic bias that has wreaked the present havoc. For years the technocrats in power insisted that distribution would follow growth. Others claim that income distribution produces a distribution of gross product. They ignore the fact that this correlation depends on the relation between domestic and external prices and on the economy's technical coefficients.

Starting in the 1950s, all countries in the Third World began to elaborate their economic development plans. They always contained a chapter on health and a chapter on education. But these social chapters were merely designed to educate and improve the population in order to smoothe the way to economic development. In the chapter on education, literacy campaigns, primary and secondary education, technical training and university courses were cited as stepping stones to economic development. In a segregated society, however, education and health for the dispossessed masses have no direct impact on economic growth.

In the long run, of course, no society develops or becomes truly democratic unless it educates its masses, but the long term has never found its way into such development plans. The justification for educating the masses, based on the exigencies of economic growth, had its source in the hypocrisy of the planners, who either acted to placate public opinion or at the pricking of a guilty conscience, or else in their incompetence in putting forward proposals that failed to tally with their purposes.

Purely social investments, especially in countries with large, destitute populations like Brazil, should be guided solely by ethical considerations and implemented by political will; they should not be made for the sake of economic maximization. At present, social investments are self-justifying (despite often entailing hefty economic investment) on account of their opportunity costs, or else are simply not justified. Mass literacy campaigns, for example, do not raise gross product, except through a tenuous relation to productivity when the newly-literate population joins the workforce. Economic growth can be secured by training a small section of the population directly involved in industrial production. This is why developing countries have invested proportionately greater sums in higher education and training for the workforce than in basic education. Social investments have always been made from the crumbs of available funds left over after economic infrastructure projects and overtly productive sectors have had their fill.

The way to solve social problems is to draft economic expediency into the service of social objectives. This can be done by setting targets to be met in the fields of health, education and sanitation as key goals in the social process and by trimming the sails of economic ordinances to the trade winds of their needs. This will never be feasible if the economy is administered on economic principles. The economy has a natural bias – whatever the political inclinations of those running it may be – towards viewing social problems from the point of view of production, employment and distribution, instead of coming to grips with their essence, which is the founding of a harmonious society where culture evolves through the quest to broaden the horizon of freedom.

A dynamic economy is vital to achieving this purpose, but it must be a means and not an end in itself. It must be subordinate to and conditioned by social objectives and not *vice versa*, as has been the case in recent decades when social concerns have been relegated to the sidelines by the exacting fetish of economic growth.

Cosmopolitan nationalism

One cannot envisage a people's future without examining it against the backdrop of international integration and the trend towards abolishing frontiers. In this sense, Brazil is a backward country. It conserves all the disadvantages of absolute but sadly dependent integration and the drawbacks of exaggerated protectionism that severs its links with the outside world. Viewing the future from the standpoint of integration does not, however, mean instantly scrapping economic frontiers to suit the same élite that has grown fat under the wing of dependent protectionism, so enabling it to grow even richer and further segregate the population through a combination of international integration and national disintegration. This would entail presenting what is actually an illusory, socially deformed modernity in the guise of protection-free integration.

During the 1970s, developed countries, faced with a glut of financial liquidity, persuaded developing countries to accept loans that later filled the banks' safes to bursting and further impoverished the debtor countries. The 1980s demonstrated that this road was in fact a dead-end and weakened these countries' international standing, bringing them to the brink of bankruptcy. The 1990s will surely see an about-turn in priorities. Developed nations will urge poor countries to purchase advanced technology and embark on a new wave of economic liberalism as unsuited to their future as the loans of the 1970s. In poor countries, many economists and public figures will defend the purchase of such technologies and the dismantling of frontiers in the name of modernization, just as those contracting loans had done in the 1970s. If this policy is to be adopted without being subjected to the greater interests of an efficient, harmonious society, the consequences that will surface in the first or second decade of the 21st century will be every bit as devastating as the havoc wreaked by external debt.

It has taken forty years of constant evolution in countries with similar degrees of development to forge European integration. They refrained from integrating in the immediate post-war period when many were still in ruins, and even later when a number of European countries had much more solid economies. They gradually nurtured closer ties through a cautious strategy designed to iron out the differences between them before embarking on integration.

The world is bound for international integration, but this must not be raised to the status of yet another economic fetish. Those who leap to the defence of international integration as a means of conquering new markets overlook the fact that many Third World countries have to cope with millions who have not been integrated into their domestic markets. These integrationists are keen, for instance, to see Brazil join international blocs before it has itself formed a 150 million-strong domestic bloc. They seek to integrate Brazil with the outside world before it has integrated itself. Parts of Brazil are far more segregated from each other than the modern part of the country is in relation to the rest of the world. Integration that disregards the majority of the population and the country's domestic potential will only aggravate domestic inequalities, igniting the powder-keg of social revolt and sending integration up in a cloud of smoke.

The international integration espoused by neo-liberalism will foster a sort of international apartheid that splits national societies in two: the rich and modern linked to their counterparts around the world, and the poor, isolated and incapable of associating with their brethren.

It is impossible to subordinate the economy to social concerns through integration with international capital. This is unworkable simply because capital's obvious interest is in maximizing profits by reproducing in developing countries the economic model minted abroad. However, several economists believe this to be the solution, since integration would gradually enable the Brazilian population to attain the level of consumption in rich countries. All their problems would then be solved by development.

This attitude can only be explained by a total lack of social commitment to the country or by a failure to grasp the simplest arithmetic of social accounting. Given the present state of technological development, the high standard of consumption in developed countries and among the wealthy in poor countries will perpetuate the impoverishment of the majority and the ecological imbalance for a good many decades.

Integrating Brazil's poor into the world economy would require a stock of capital that is simply not available in the modern world. Extending this to other poor countries would only make it even less possible to achieve.

All countries that nowadays display a greater degree of development at some point in the past opted for assertion of their nationality by taking an independent, autonomous stand. The best example of the theoretical economic analysis which inspired this approach is to be found in the work of the German economist Friedrich List who, in the mid-19th century, formulated the idea of a national economy, in contrast to the cosmopolitanism of Adam Smith which then held sway among European theorists.

Economists' ignorance of history compounds the bias of their approach due to the natural disdain they feel for home-grown options. Nevertheless, despite the existence of similar development patterns, there is no reason to suggest that each country should adopt precisely the same model as those that have already undergone development. Any solution for social development must necessarily contain a specific national outlook and design. This includes national sentiment forged by awareness of the population's common purposes, and dignity in the handling and use of local resources.

New nationalism must also be viewed and understood in its international dimension. It would be ridiculous to imagine a state of the 21st century living in splendid isolation from the rest of the world, just as it would be misleading to claim that the road to progress lies in disregarding the nation's specific characteristics.

The world is clearly bound for integration, and those countries, like Brazil, that are already party to the international system cannot now retreat into isolation. What is needed is firm nationalism that will autonomously set out the purposes of and uses to which natural resources are to be put. At the same time, however, this nationalism must be cosmopolitan enough not to ignore the current trend towards integration and the advantages that may be derived from it. We need nationalism to raise questions about the desired future of the nation; we need cosmopolitanism to search the world for the technical answers.

Cosmopolitan nationalism embraces the following premises:

(1) Believing in and desiring constant international integration.

(2) Being aware that this does not mean aping today's rich countries; on the contrary, it implies endeavouring to realize that, if Brazil's resources and ecological riches are well used, it is those rich countries that will soon be clamouring for integration.

(3) Not wanting to 'reinvent the wheel', but being equally aware that it is not worth being run over by the wheels invented abroad just because they happen to work or look good.

(4) Understanding that if there are shared problems, objectives and resources as well as neutral technologies, there are also differing problems, objectives and resources as well as technologies that are not in the least neutral since they produce effects that vary according to the society and natural environment in which they are implemented.

(5) Realizing that social results are the fruit not only of resources and technology but also of the sovereignty with which they are handled.

(6) Understanding that the power of technologies demands great responsibility of each country in its use of available national resources and techniques.

The technology of technology

The endeavour to promote modernization is a permanent commitment of any society. Throughout history this has meant striving to build a healthy, competent society which provides its members with access to technical knowledge attuned to tomorrow's requirements. It is a constant process of transforming minerals, plants and animals into people and their by-products, fulfilling a constantly evolving project of civilization.

It is ridiculous to think that at the threshold of the 21st century, when a clear awareness and prospect of an integrated planet are beginning to emerge, a country can successfully pursue technological isolation.

Each civilization has prevailed in its time by commanding the leading-edge technologies of the day, and the future will demand the same of every society. One should not, however, confuse this command of technology with the purchase of black boxes designed to meet artificially induced needs.

The Industrial Revolution has distorted the meaning of the expression 'technological control', especially in this century. Instead of meaning mastery of knowledge for solving social problems, technological control now means the power to employ a particular technique at society's disposal, regardless of whether it is in society's interest. The upshot of this is that, rather than being an instrument of social liberation, technological control has become an instrument of social domination. This predicament is all the more acute in dependent societies where consumption standards are copied down to the last detail, regardless of their social consequences. This feeble mimicry is dubbed technological advance. When this occurs, these countries are brought under the thumb of a technical advance they neither comprehend nor command.

Technical advances for building a healthy future should be divided into two sorts: first, the power to control the use of techniques for the purposes of bringing about the society one desires; secondly, the power to master each technique, discovering how it operates and gaining access to its use. The former type of control is political, the latter technical.

By adopting, *a priori*, the definition of modernity as the utilization of leading-edge technology, most economists are duped by a mirage of modernity. They fail to separate political control of technologies (technical control of their engineering) from access to techniques. What matters is, first, that we should control technology by making it serve a modernization plan based on socially-determined standards and objectives; secondly, that we should master the technical know-how required to create this and not simply gain access to the use of technology by buying it in. One can only begin to talk of technological modernity when both types of control occur.

Another pitfall that has beguiled many economists is that of being over-awed at new techniques, taking them to be techniques for the future. Not all new techniques are actually modern. Technical modernity must come fine-tuned to the essence of the objectives of modernity. This delusion is the reason why economists all too often justify access – in the name of modernity – to technologies that hinder rather than hasten the modernity they yearn for. One instance of this is the purchase of technologies that harm society, plunge the country deep into debt, and maim its prospects – quite the opposite of modernization. The countries of the Third World are eloquent examples of this back-to-front mirage where technical advance is confused with the purchase of contraptions geared to imitative consumption standards wholly unrelated to society's real needs. Many of these playthings are unsuited to or even at odds with available resources. At best this condemns them to the scrap-heap; at worst it provokes social upheaval.

Isolation is not an option. Besides being impossible in the long run, isolation would conflict with the objective of increasing society's global heritage. On the other hand, the facts demonstrate that it is an error to imagine that one can increase society's store of wealth by uncontrolled exposure to technological innovation, as the First World's cosmopolitan economists have been proposing for the last two hundred years – a position many Third World economists have since accepted. Prisoners of cultural colonialism, incapable of fielding their own theoretical models, these economists fail to come up with alternatives that combine foreign technologies and national interests without lapsing into cringing subservience or foolhardy xenophobia. They insist on the idea of a single, autonomous process of technological advance for the entire globe and envisage each country throwing wide its doors in the expectation that the effects will be a blessing to society as a whole.

The solution is not to turn a blind eye to the negative effects of uncontained importation of poorly-adapted technologies. Nor is it to resort to unworkable, undesirable isolationism. Rather, it is to regulate the mechanism of innovation, creating interaction between all technologies, united by a rationale that will subordinate technology to the greater goal of building up society's global heritage and wealth.[3]

Notes

1. Data quoted from the statistical appendices in Marcelo de Paiva Abreu's *A Ordem do Progresso* <The order of progress>, Rio de Janeiro, Ed. Campus, 1989.

2. Hélio Jaguaribe *et al.*, *Brasil, Reforma ou Caos* <Brazil, reform or chaos>, São Paulo, Ed. Paz e Terra, 1989, p. 60.

3. For an analysis of this issue, with concrete proposals regarding means of achieving adequate technological adaptation, see Cristovam Buarque & Sergio C. Buarque, *Tecnologia Apropriada: Una Política para la Banca de Desarrollo*, Lima, ALIDE, 1983.

CHAPTER 5

Economic Fetishism

Masking reality

When oil prices were rocketing, a high-ranking official in the Saudi Arabian government declared that his country's most serious problem was that every time they drilled a well for water, oil gushed to the surface. Like other oil-producing countries in the Middle East, Saudi Arabia was experiencing the drama of the Phrygian King Midas who, in exchange for liberating the satyr Silenus, was granted the gift of turning everything he touched to gold. Stunned by the possibilities of his new power, Midas only realized the snag when he sat down to his first meal.

Modern economists still work in ignorance of the myth of Midas and deprived of the experience of the Saudi official. It is this ignorance that will lead them to think that the world is richer the day after the death of the last surviving elephant because the price of ivory goes up.

The refinement of economic models projects the gains of speculators years in advance yet fails to mask the fragility of a theory that considers the death of the last elephant a positive phenomenon. These models conceal an absurd situation under the cloak of a fetish trumped up by economic theory.

Of all the distortions that the developmentalist approach has brought to understanding the social process, the most serious is the way the quandary of civilization has been transformed into an economic dilemma. This deformity becomes all the more insidious as it affects the entire tissue of society, which then begins to regard itself as a mirror of the economy. Social problems and those directly associated with the essence of human dealings are stripped of their identity and engulfed by the monolithic reality of the economy. Misled by years of economic primacy, society has been enveigled into regarding economic problems as the real nuts to be cracked. Malnutrition and the lack of education and culture are demoted as priority concerns, nuisances such as external debt, inflation, the energy crisis and interest rates being billed as the basic problems. By inverting values in this way, society gets out of touch with reality and flounders in the search for a solution to its real problems.

When an efficient socio-economic model faces mild crises, this approach may help to provide a resumption of growth and improvement in well-being. But when the crisis is grafted onto the model itself, quelling it requires more profound reforms that can never take place while reasoning remains shackled to the fetishist outlook.

By acting on the basis of fetishist principles of this kind, economists are at the same time submitting to and legitimizing a rationale woven on the loom of prevailing yet archaic ideologies. These ideologies could have been legitimate when economic power was too small to have a hand in the extinction of animals and when such extinction was neither predictable nor manageable as a feature of economic values. By preserving the values of such ideologies and disregarding the ethical consequences that issue from economic acts, economists forge a rationale that serves as an ideological curtain for masking and shutting out reality.

By explaining the world and its relations in a way that suits the prevailing ideology, economic theory legitimizes the absurd and the irrational. A country's biggest bumper harvest is thus hailed as a resounding success story regardless of the hunger of millions it does nothing to assuage. For it is more profitable to export agricultural produce as fodder for animals reared to make delicacies for the refined palates of the fortunate few. The medical equipment industry can be a thriving business whether or not it helps to allay the suffering caused by illness. The greatest literary works are gauged by the aggregate value of their sales. By seeking to quantify and then restricting the value of things to this quantification, Economics operates with mythical variables that disguise reality, moulding it to fit a particular logic and a specific purpose.

In contrast to explanatory myths, the myths of economic theory are designed for intervention. In his analyses of Keynesian theory, the Brazilian economist, Professor Lauro Campos, demonstrates that this masking of reality is specifically designed to kindle the dynamics of production.[1]

Given the irrational framework within which the economy operates, Economics is compelled to fabricate myths that will persuade people to judge clearly absurd patterns of behaviour to be rational. In their thirst for liberation, people would react so strongly to much of the labour structure, demands and output of the economy that the only way to induce them to work would be to contrive an imaginary world where a particular species of logic motivates people and explains reality to them. At the same time as they strive to make the economy operational, economists conjure up a reality apart, impelled by a special rationale cast as the dynamo of the economic process.

Occasionally reality emerges from behind the veil of ideology and reveals its true colours to a stunned world, and the theories of the day are forced to capitulate to this rebellion. However, new explanations rapidly arise, raising the curtain on one side and hastily screening off other unseemly parts of upstart reality. Just as there is a plethora of scholastic intellectual lucubrations aimed at reshaping the world as viewed by science and making it match prevailing dogmas, examples of the phantasmagoria of economic models abound.

This is not merely a breakdown in Keynesian thinking, however. All introductions to Economics define the economic dilemma as being how to 'satisfy infinite needs with scarce resources'. But this concept has been formulated without economists ever having discussed the concept of needs or considered scarcity as a real fact. This slipshod definition (based on pre-determined, partial premises) accounts for the shortcomings of Economics in explaining the workings of the modern world.

Scarcity is treated as a straightforward, short-term imbalance in price structures caused by the supply/demand equation. The demand for end-products and inputs is held to be absolutely unrelated to real needs, which do not even rank among economic concepts. Meanwhile, analysis of basic inputs, especially natural resources, is confined to the matter of pricing, which is wholly unrelated to the real exhaustion of these resources. Theory posits that scarcity contains the instruments for remedying itself. These mechanisms consist in magic elasticities that automatically raise the output of products and resources or replace them whenever their prices rise beyond determined levels.

This is one of the weak points of the economistic outlook. It is especially noticeable during moments of crisis when reality is stripped bare and theories prove incapable of glossing over it. When technical advances can achieve surplus production and large sectors of the population are still afflicted by food shortages, the equilibrium theory fails to satisfy social conscience, putting moderately sensitive economists to shame. The argument that it is best to dump or destroy produce when prices are unattractive rather than using it to feed the starving is unconvincing. Likewise, the idea of automatic substitution of natural resources is not easy to swallow when one observes the growing demand for these resources at the present level of worldwide consumption. The theory of automatic replaceability of products and factors is based on an elegant, even rigorous logical formulation worthy of the scholastics. It is, none the less, a subjective logic that will not stand up to the slightest probing by ethical values nor bear any exposure to reality.

Like the replaceability of resources theory, many economic phenomena fail to withstand empirical verification. Economics, which emerged in the wake of the empiricists' quest for knowledge from the 17th century onwards, has not experimented as much as it would like. To overcome this hurdle, Economics has created a world of imaginary concepts which look sufficient in themselves and are justified by logical verification instrinsic to the very models they created to explain human behaviour and social relations, regardless of reality.

By unquestioningly accepting its logical foundations as irrefutable truths, the science of Economics has invented variables, coefficients, indicators, and a language capable of veiling reality. Taking its status as a science for granted, Economics has forged a theoretical framework that approximates to a theology of the production process. Like all theologies, Economics was founded on dogmas which constitute its basic premises.

The limitations of economists stem from their refusal to analyse the economic process on a human basis that would unshackle their science from the premises of the prevailing socio-political system. Unlike physical sciences, which have merely rediscovered the need for regulatory ethics, Economics must incorporate ethical principles as premises that are an integral part of its models for explaining reality. Atoms have no morals; economic agents do. If the economy does not solve the problem of hunger, theoretical models should not describe the agricultural policy as being successful. If market profits cause the extinction of an animal species, the economy's global product measured by economists should surely reflect this fact.

That it does not yet do so is because economists refuse to include in their theories, models and interpretations the changes that the world in which the economic process is unfolding undergoes from day to day with regard to a number of basic aspects of the human condition. Since the 19th century, economists have assumed that the object of their study has its own life, separate from nature and from culture. To them the object possesses an omnipotent technological potential and, with slight modifications, is capable of adjusting to new circumstances without altering its core objective. The next step was to imagine that the dynamics of the economic system were the mainspring of universal history, as well as natural history, which could then be manipulated to suit the economic interests of the human race.

As justification for such behaviour, Pareto pointed out that to find his way on the high seas a navigator does not need to know about the evolution of the continents and oceans down the millions of years of geological time; all he needs to know is some geography and the coordinates of navigation. Georgescu-Roegen contests this traditional view – a view consciously or unconsciously shared by the great majority of economists – by stating that 'Pareto's illustration is baseless since geographical evolution is nothing like as fast as change in the world of Economics'.[2] If the navigator had to travel for millions of years, then he too would have to take stock of geological transformations.

Most economists hold that the object of study in Economics does not change. Theory serves as a map for finding one's way and achieving understanding. It evolves in terms of perfecting the portrait it paints of the workings of the economic process. Economists are like cartographers who update their maps to include hitherto unrecorded or unnoticed features, but who never introduce substantial changes to the face of the earth. Such slight alterations as they do allow, economists proudly justify in terms of the re-equilibrating mechanisms Marshall described. It was on these mechanisms that Pareto based his short-term 'Marshallian' theory, according to which, when the earthquakes and tidal waves had subsided, the economy would swiftly settle back into its old routine.

The science of Economics would thus evolve to keep pace with the economy, just as Medicine, Astronomy and Physics had evolved since prehistory, though the objects of their study (the human body, celestial bodies, the physical world) had undergone no major changes.

The relation between the economy and the science that studies it is in fact entirely different. The irregular pattern of change demands a science that evolves fast enough to detect it. Moreover, in the case of Economics, the scientist is part of the object of his study. As Godelier

puts it: 'Providing social sciences examine any problem at a sufficiently general level, the social scientist stands within the radius,
which means that the researcher is himself part of the society he sets
out to study, which plays an important part in the elaboration of the
intellectual categories employed.'[3] By shutting themselves off from
the transformations that are constantly taking place in society, economists adopt a merely interpretative, partial approach to the workings
of the status quo. They take certain dogmas and, detaching their
concepts from the facts of the mutable reality they should be taking
pains to scrutinize, defend interests camouflaged under the guise of
'scientific objectivity'. They ignore the fact that the few who actually
have access to 'economic freedom' have employed it to enslave the
remainder; they behave like the Greeks who waxed eloquent about
liberty while being carried on the shoulders of slaves. Under the veil
of the term 'efficiency', they fail to take stock of the ecological and
social disasters that such activity sponsors.

'The question,' says Georgescu, 'is why science, which is interested
in the means, purposes and distribution, should dogmatically refuse to
examine the process by which new economic means, new purposes
and new economic relations are created?'[4]

The reply is to be found in an analysis of the different groups of
economists:

(1) Those consciously concerned to avoid any change in premises and
objectives.

(2) Those who are neither interested in nor capable of grasping the
essence of the process, nor in a position to assume ethical values that
would redefine the premises of the science since their knowledge is
restricted to analyses of theoretical models.

(3) Those who are not content with the straight-jacket of the prevailing
ideology and opt for a different approach based on a new ideology
grounded in the interests of new classes.

(4) Other intellectuals, not always recognized as economists by their
would-be colleagues, who seek a new explanation for the phenome-
nology of the process of transforming minerals, plants and animals
into men and their by-products.

At the end of a chapter on Adam Smith, Mark Blaug writes: 'In reviewing Smith or any other economist, we should always remember that brilliance in handling pure analytical concepts is a very different thing from a firm grasp of the essential logic of economic relations.'[5]

This comment could well apply to the technocracy schooled and groomed during the last three decades to administer the capitalist state in developing countries. The extraordinary weight of analytical data with which they have been primed prevents them from learning, thinking and understanding the heart of the economic process. They cannot detach themselves from the premises that legitimize the prevailing framework and have grown incapable of criticizing the essence of the process. They are incapacitated for the ethical revolution that would otherwise enable them to propose radical changes in the objectives of economic policy. They are confined to juggling the variables without ever asking what their real significance may be or contesting the pre-determined aims of Economics, much less the morals implicit in the formulations of economic policy. Joan Robinson makes a similar criticism of the training economists have received during this period, claiming that learning mathematics has, for many of them, meant losing the power to think. What she means is that mathematical language, which can be of great help in articulating understanding, operates on the basis of pre-determined premises. So, if an economist is confined to this language, he will obviously not be able to undertake ethical criticism of the objectives it aims to accomplish. He cannot conceive a real world existing beyond the scope of the models prefabricated to the specifications established by mathematical reasoning. Daniel Boorstin makes a similar point about the great 19th-century physicist Michael Faraday when he says that the revolutionary notion of fields of force, which defies common sense, could never have been imagined by a scientist bound up in traditional models: 'If Faraday had been grounded in mathematics, he would not have been prepared for his surprising novel view of the world.'[6]

So long as it continues to operate without a more critical attitude towards its underlying rationale and language, even if it does change its ideological standards, Economics will remain wrapped up in myths and fetishes. This epistemological prison is a hallmark of all systems of thinking that are tethered to the language they create. In physical sciences, however, this prison is an undetected phenomenon of which the scientist himself is unaware. Linguistic limitations are chanced upon when a new language is shaped. In Economics, on the other hand, it is the maintenance of incomplete, imperfect concepts that betrays this limitation. The presupposition of ethical neutrality in Economics makes it a prisoner of its own language even though it acknowledges the existence of the prison. The notion of needs is then confounded with the idea of demand. The multitude starving for want of wages are of no import if prices are kept neatly in balance with the level of available income. There will be no supply shortages if the needy can be extricated from the columns of demand statistics through lack of purchase power. The concept of value, meanwhile, flatly ignores the effect of depredation on the environment.

Throughout the world, technocratic economists have chosen to distance themselves from the political reality that has served as the basis for implementing their strategies. They have not hesitated to resort to police repression, torture and the abolition of all forms of liberty as instruments of economic policy. This evinces a two-fold lack of ethics: through disrespect for basic human values during dictatorships; through subsequent denials, in periods when democracy is being reinstated, of authoritarian commitment to the military whom they served as accomplices.[7] To this must be added a grave epistemological impropriety in their refusal to acknowledge the use of such instruments among the tools and methods of economic policy.

The problem is not that economists have not learnt their lessons well in the courses they attended; it is that that they have learnt them much as a chemist learns what substances to mix to obtain sodium bicarbonate, without asking themselves why, what for, and at what cost. In studying their science as something unrelated to the realities of their countries, economists have lost the perspective for understanding the essence of the economic process and keeping abreast of the mutable reality in which this process unfolds. Economists have thus become a species of cardinals of a church, whose brief it is to set out the arguments that justify current dogma. In so doing, they bear out the criticisms explicitly levelled at them by Georgescu-Roegen when he states that: 'As a result of the modern belief that industrial development is the panacea for all ills, every developing country is now bent on developing to the teeth, without pausing to consider whether or not it possesses within its frontiers the natural resources it requires.'[8] Worse still is the fact that when reality fails to confirm their predictions, they manipulate statistics and trump up a new reality, divorced from real facts but better suited to their theories. This sort of flaw is not the preserve of economists but permeates the entire network that constitutes modern bureaucracy in every country the world over.[9]

What differentiates and aggravates the position of economists in relation to other bureaucrats (such as members of the armed forces and the health service) is that they have played a leading role in plotting the course to be taken by society and civilization as a whole. Hobbled and blinkered by their language, their theories and the false data they manipulate, economists have not managed to get civilization and society back on the rails. Likewise, they have failed to rid themselves of myths and fetishes or to pinpoint and correctly define the problems that need to be tackled to permit full understanding of the economy in its relation to human essence. They have neglected to subordinate the economy to the greater cause of human liberation in which the provision of goods and services would be little more than important means.

Economists thus behave like ballistics technicians attempting to plot the trajectory of a projectile on the basis of the hypothetical force of another planet's gravity without considering data about drag and without bothering about the effects its collision may cause.

One cannot, of course, tar all those concerned with Economics with the brush of technocratic alienation so rife in the Third World. The Brazilian economist Celso Furtado begins his book *Prefácio à Nova Economia Política* with the following sentence: 'A quarter of a century spent probing the labyrinths of economic theories and striving to pick out the relations between the teachings that derive from them and the practical problems of our time has thoroughly convinced me of the inadequacy of the conceptual framework we operate with in this science.'[10] An economist who makes such a statement cannot be lumped in with those who can do no better than an alienated interpretation of reality. Like Furtado, other economists (both within and beyond the walls of academia) have been expressing deep concern at the results and imperfections of the models employed.

These 'other economists' have not yet come up with an alternative proposal. Celso Furtado himself points out that his text is an itinerary for seeking new foundations for an alternative economic science to replace the classical formulations that survive to the present day.

These alternative economists can be roughly divided into two groups: those devoted to critical analysis of capitalism who have no intention of coming to grips with it or proposing alternatives; and those whose perplexity makes them relapse into a nihilistic sentiment that no new instrument can possibly crack the conundrum.

The first group includes thousands of economists who have lived in the capitalist world devoting themselves to studies of Marxist theory. They undertake increasingly sophisticated interpretations of the same object of study, continually seeking to confirm the principles Marx elaborated a hundred years ago. They attempt to demonstrate how the concept of class war in nascent 19th-century European capitalism can explain the evolution of civilizations as disparate as those of medieval China, the Incas and the Aztecs. Some are no doubt bracing themselves to apply the same principles to the first extra-terrestrial civilization that makes its alien presence felt. Those who come closest to the real world apply these principles to the analysis of capitalism and its origins but show not the slightest interest in its more immediate evolution, nor do they bother about its consequences for the world, the nation and the masses. They refuse outright to have a hand in what they call 'administering the crisis' that they claim does not belong to them. This refusal alienates them from the real world. By devoting their energies to dissecting a system that is still alive and has growing chances of survival, they fall foul of the trap primed by capitalism. In fact, by accepting salaries for researching theories that neither aggregate knowledge nor alter reality, they act like pieces on the Keynesian chessboard (instruments for boosting effective demand) engaged in unproductive labour. This makes for non-commitment to reality. They hold that the only way to change the socio-economic status quo is by global revolution which they (incompetently) believe is around the corner or (irresponsibly) claim to be no concern of theirs.

Though this stance has the advantage of enabling one to interpret the historical essence of capitalism, it scarcely helps to understand present reality, nor does it help to determine the social cost of industrial growth. It also alienates a sizeable clutch of competent intellectuals in the battle against the present crisis that threatens not only the bourgeoisie and imperialism but civilization as a whole.

Such economists are incapable of making a break *within* the prevailing economic system in an endeavour to transform it; they are bound to interpretations that Marx himself would consider out-dated in modern capitalism. In striving to uphold orthodoxy, they refuse to examine a new reality: a surplus value distributed to co-opt larger segments which constitute new 'classes' of interests (albeit minority ones) among national populations; a process of international integration combined with national disintegration; a proletarian élite that has united throughout the world in a spirit of consumption-oriented (as opposed to revolutionary) fervour; predatory behaviour on a global scale producing contradictions that are perhaps even more dramatic than those of social dialectics; a simmering desire for reforms brimming over into open discontent with socialism. Incapable of advancing their knowledge of reality, as Marx did over a century ago, these economists also shirk the task of analysing the immediate situation, of finding solutions for a worldwide crisis afflicting all mankind. They prefer to pore over class struggle in the Andes at the time of the Incas instead of attempting to come to grips with what is now at stake in Peruvian society, where reality defies all existing theories and models. When they do actually have a bash at tackling the present, many prefer to falsify reality so as to adapt it to the classical texts rather than helping the theory to advance on the basis of new circumstances that emerge from one day to the next.

In Brazil's case, while traditional economists concentrate on attributing the crisis of Brazilian society to economic stumbling blocks, many Marxist theoreticians go to the opposite extreme of disdaining the hunt for solutions to immediate difficulties because, as they see it, these are but the symptoms of a wider global crisis and, as such, do not deserve separate analysis. Besides, these academics tend to be purists and so mistake what is possible in a given historical period for what is desirable in a social structure that cannot always be attained in the medium term. The end result is that when revolutionary political groups eventually take up the reins of government (whatever power structure may have placed them in command) they end up seeking support among the same technocrats who have grown accustomed to the traditional approach.

Social evolution in many underdeveloped countries in recent years has revealed this sort of behaviour on the part of critical economists who are none the less alienated by their lack of concern with reality. When they have been able to bring their influence to bear on those in power, they have resorted to the same premises that the technocrats of authoritarian regimes employed. They have proved to be poorly prepared for finding alternatives.

In Brazil's case, the predicament is all the more acute because the entire present generation of economists has been cloned from a single theoretical matrix which, knitting Marxists and neo-classical economists together, has created a web of mutual theoretical solidarity. During the dictatorship this web was split in two: the economic liberals serving political authoritarianism who strive to achieve wealth-concentrating growth; and the political liberals who defend income distribution for attaining social justice.* With the advent of democracy, one perceives an atmosphere of interaction and solidarity throughout the entire network. A good example of this is the reaction of economists of the most diverse tendencies to the various economic plans implemented in Brazil. Discrepancies have been confined to details and technical aspects, rarely representing clearly distinct concepts of the objects analysed.

The second group, the 'perplexed' economists, despite their scepticism about the feasibility of any theory, and in spite of their attempts to combine virtually irreconcilable long-term concerns with immediate solutions, do at least hold out the prospect of alternatives for understanding the reality of the economic process and determining its future evolution. The difficulties do not help them. They cannot clearly make out what is going to happen in the immediate future nor are they certain what solution to put forward for overcoming the twin crises in the real and conceptual worlds. They acknowledge the fixed contours of reality and its models but judge the dominant political base to be too strong for modifications to be made to the status quo. They thus relapse into perplexed apathy, torn between their doubts as to whether to subscribe to a revolution that stands little chance of success, to have a conniving hand in administering the crisis, or to acquiesce in the tragedy of withholding their contribution to solving a crisis that transcends governments and imposes a heavy burden on the country and the people.

There is yet a third group that makes a clean break with the prevailing scheme of things and proffers radical alternatives. Its members espouse an idealist option, wholly attuned to nature, or cling to the opportunism of an authoritarian economic solution, along the lines of real socialism.

Ecological romanticism, by entirely rejecting the possibility of efficiently substituting truly scarce natural resources without upsetting the balance of nature, reveals itself to be the reflex of another

---

* Translator's note: Brazil was governed by a military dictatorship from 1964 to 1985.

theological form. It artificially removes the human race from the centre of the natural process, ignores the social costs implicit in a conservationist stance, and sinks back into a religious mode, instating a green God.

Those who continue to rally round the flag of real socialism fail to perceive the very real economic and social fragility it has shown. On the economic front, centralization has proved deficient. Economies that have satisfactorily cured social sores and mastered advanced technology have been incapable of catering for the population's consumption needs. Two features cause these deficiencies: the un-workability of the techniques for managing the millions of variables that make up the economic process; and the difficulty of combining individual incentives with equality. Equality, moreover, is incapable of furnishing the sophisticated, expensive goods for which society clamours. On the social front, the outward equality attained by the system has roused dissatisfaction and prompted systemic malfunctions, above all in a world of internationally integrated information networks and glaringly dissimilar consumption patterns. The transformations that have occurred in the Soviet Union and other Eastern European countries are ready instances of this fact. They had to quell a veritable rebellion stirred up by the smouldering desire for individual freedom and by comparison of consumer standards in socialist and capitalist countries in Europe. They have also had to cope with dissatisfaction at the distribution of luxury goods promoted by state intervention rather than market forces.

Coming to terms with magic

The endeavours Economics has made and the advances it has achieved have failed to make economic reality easier to understand. The more knowledge advances, the more complex reality becomes. In a way, the epistemological gap between economic theories and reality widens with the passage of time. Aristotle's world was better matched to the formulations of his thought than is today's mercurial world to contemporary economic models.

In spite of all its shortcomings and weaknesses, Economics is the social science that can best contribute to understanding the relations between individuals and between the human race and nature. That is why it is of the utmost importance that Economics should rid itself of its dogmatic prejudices and its alienation from reality. Economists who see themselves as exact scientists and the defenders of a positive economy should take a good look at our changing natural and social environment. On the basis of their findings, they can then formulate models that unite people in productive joint action, improving their interaction with each other and with nature.

Those who devote themselves to what is known as political economy should delve deep into the problems of the day. These include both problems that derive from the dynamics of modern civilization and problems that are peculiar to the countries in which they live and work. They should relinquish the habit of concentrating their studies on autopsies of capitalism, since there is every indication that this system will remain alive and kicking for many decades yet. The autopsies of socialism in which some are now gleefully engrossed should likewise be eschewed.

Finally, one must realize that 'economic analysis' has overlooked essential ingredients in the process, such as the value of nature, the long-term perspective, and the cultural values of each people. It has continued to nurture an optimistic outlook founded on a belief in the omnipotence of technology to solve all problems – including those it creates. A redefinition of the functions of production, incorporating the entropic effect of economic activities, may produce analytical instruments that can graft onto economic theory a new rationale, equipping it to make the break with theology and become a full-blown science of relations between humankind and nature.

It will be the brief of this new science to delve into that which lies behind the veil of ideologically determined premises and venture forth in search of the essence of the economy. At the same time, one must envisage this search as being free to range beyond a mechanistic, positivist or materialist-historical approach. It must be receptive to the sense of magic that resides in the economic process: the magic that stands behind inexplicable objectives and methods; the magic of organized undertakings that concentrate efforts (which mean time in lives) to get us to the moon, to erect pyramids in the desert, to stage a carnival or religious procession, or to raise consumption; the magic capable of mounting the logistical apparatus for a state to wage war and the private-sector logistics that make it possible to supply a megalopolis.

This magic consists in thousands of years of physical and intellectual labour expended by people who, throughout history, have united, liaised and complemented each other on the basis of laws they cannot fathom, laws that will never be intelligible if we remain tied up in prejudice and incapable of acknowledging that there is magic at the frontiers of our knowledge. The attempt to grapple with it is in itself a magical objective that is justified not merely by increased efficiency in attaining the essence of the civilizational process but also because it is an aesthetic objective. This is true regardless of any reason other than the aesthetic value of the quest, provided it is guided by ethical principles that aim at the extension and use of freedom – even in order to go in search of the truth.

Notes

1. See Lauro Campos, *A Crise da Ideologia Keynesiana* <The crisis of Keynesian ideology>, Rio de Janeiro, Ed. Campus, 1982.

2. N. Georgescu-Roegen, *The Entropy Law and the Economic Process*, Cambridge, Mass., Harvard University Press, 1971, p. 320. Georgescu refers to the economist Vilfredo Pareto and to the theory of equilibrium propounded by another neo-classical theoretician, Alfred Marshall.

3. L. Godelier, *Épistemologie et Philosophie Politique*, Paris, Éditions Denoel-Gouthier, 1978, p. 23.

4. Georgescu-Roegen, *op. cit.*, p. 320.

5. Mark Blaug, *Economic Theory in Retrospect*, 3rd ed. London, Cambridge University Press, 1978, p. 65.

6. Daniel Boorstin, *The Discoverers: A History of Man's Search to Know His World and Himself*, Harmondsworth, Penguin Books, 1983, p. 679.

7. The author has dealt with this issue in non-academic form in two works of political satire: *A Ressureição do General Sanchez* <The resurrection of General Sanchez>, Rio de Janeiro, Ed. Civilização Brasileira, 1981 (especially the chapter entitled 'A Catedral do Diabo' <The devil's cathedral>) and *A Eleição do Ditador* <Electing the dictator>, São Paulo, Ed. Paz e Terra, 1988.

8. Georgescu-Roegen, *op. cit.*, p. 293.

9. It is worth consulting D. Halbertram's book *The Best and the Brightest* (Conn., Fawcett Crest Books, 1973) on the way the brilliant team appointed by John Kennedy's administration manipulated information and so committed a series of errors.

10. Celso Furtado, *Prefácio a uma Nova Economia Política* <Preface to new political economics>, São Paulo, Ed. Paz e Terra, 1976.

CHAPTER 6

The Power of Technology

The vitality of myths

A good deal of world history consists of the myriad myths shaped by human imagination. The history of the modern world has fulfilled the prophecies of the myth of Midas, turning export crops to gold and condemning local populations to starvation. Above all, it has been the history of Prometheus and Pandora, the history of human euphoria as we unveil the world's mysteries and shed our innocence. We rejoice at the departure of ignorance and suffer from the advent of sin. We achieve the power to master the world and yet we come under its spell. We become aware of what goes on around us, we create myths, but we fail to avert the senseless, inexorable onward march of the tragedies we write. We cannot resist the temptation of Pandora's itching curiosity, Prometheus' daring, or Midas' lust. Above all, we kindle Faust's venal optimism, behaving like the Sorcerer's Apprentice.

In September 1987, an anonymous scrap-metal merchant in Brazil's Centre West was the unwitting protagonist of all these myths when he broke open a caesium-137 capsule. As Pandora, he prised open a black box full of lethal surprises. As Prometheus, he cupped in his hands the fire that belonged to little glowing gods. As Midas, he contaminated everything he touched. He was a Faust who sold his soul to earn his bread and discovered that this curious magic eluded his control.

He knew nothing of this. He was performing the oft-repeated, frequently morbid but eternally fascinating ritual of discovering what the things of the world contain in order to transform them into goods to do our bidding. He did not realise that, like all men, he was hostage to his own impulse. He was unaware of this because, like all people, he possessed, allied to his curiosity, a boundless sense of optimism and power.

The story of Prometheus is an allegory of the drama of the human race. It portrays the role of science in the mastery of fire with all the benefits it has had for humanity – physical liberation through the power to master hostile nature and spiritual liberation through the power of knowledge; liberation from all forms of tutelage and control by the gods.

The scientist is a modern Prometheus, constantly stealing and mastering the gods' secrets and pressing them into the service of humankind. But scientists act like children who do not know how to administer their discoveries. A similar tale is told in the classical myth of Pandora or the modern tale of the Sorcerer's Apprentice. Like a pyromaniacal Prometheus, scientists make science an end in itself, wielding stolen fire for good or ill so long as it satisfies their curiosity.

In this sense, Greek playwrights failed fully to express the incompetence of modern Prometheuses. By having the gods punish the human race for stealing knowledge, the Greeks did not envisage the ineptitude of people punishing themselves by the unthinking use of their discoveries.

One can detect a streak of rebellion in the creation and transfer of technology. On the one hand, it evolves independently of the social welfare it aims to promote and, on the other, it is beginning to produce negative side-effects, 'dis-economies', that cast a long shadow on its results. In modern production systems, technological progress is not tailored to real needs. At times, one observes the reverse of rationality. Instead of being provided with technologies designed to reduce costs, society is induced to consume new goods wrought by new technologies even if it has to pay more for the same results. The situation becomes even bleaker when the social and ecological costs are totted up. Some products are replaced by others merely to justify a novel production process, even though the end results are identical. The health system in the United States already demonstrates that the search for health has become a pretext for promoting growing industrialization, the dynamics of which depend on new equipment, whether or not it produces better results. What matters is that demand for dearer new technologies be created.

This scheme for fuelling innovation, regardless of real results, begins to stoke up a rebellion that society will find hard to control even when its uneconomic features become apparent. One such example is the automobile industry. In the early 1970s, difficulties derived from the indiscriminate use of individual transport technology began to raise their ugly heads: waste of fossil fuels, environmental contamination, high infrastructure costs and inefficient transportation on account of traffic jams. Despite this, the system does not easily adjust.

Technology creates its own dynamics. Instead of adjusting itself or being replaced by another model, prevailing technology dominates the social and economic system. It imposes higher outlay on urban infrastructure, demands subsidies, even for the development of more expensive new fuels, and forces the economy to run up a debt to import oil. Instead of replacing obsolete technologies by a more rational system, better adapted to existing circumstances, society adjusts to the new reality wrought by technology. The most obvious solution – mastering transport technology and only then deciding on the most appropriate vehicle – is brushed aside.

This occurs because technology has worked its way into the grain of the economic system. Technical advance, levered by economic demand, acquires its own momentum. Economic growth is then dictated by these inertial interests which prevent a change in habits (except those that favour further advances), sponsor interests opposed to change, and impose an outlook that hinders understanding of social needs taken separately from technical progress. Since there is a social base with interests in each technological model, the only way to master technology is by modifying the social, economic and even the psychological framework of society.

In the case of societies receiving foreign technology, the problem is aggravated by the fact that the technology imported is poorly adapted to local conditions and this causes social disintegration. As they penetrate technologically backward societies, the modern technologies created in rich countries violate such societies, forcing the socio-economic framework to bend to the new requirements. This provokes six phenomena that can increasingly be observed as the local technological model is modified by the importation of unadapted new standards:

(1) A sharp increase in external debt caused by the need to invest in technological standards based on imported natural resources, inputs and know-how.

(2) Concentration of income to buoy up domestic demand for sumptuous, expensive goods beyond the budget of the average earner.

(3) Sudden internal migrations in the rush to taste the benefits of a society modernizing at a far faster pace than would be possible if adjustments were gradually introduced.

(4) Political authoritarianism to push through policies for concentrating wealth, accumulating capital and installing an infrastructure unrelated to the interests of the majority of the population.

(5) Severe cultural disarray caused by the clash of technologically dissimilar cultures, along the lines of the ferment sowed by the era of discoveries in the 16th century.

(6) National disintegration, when a minority is integrated into a new technological world while the majority stands on the sidelines, saddled with handling backward techniques and subsisting peripherally in primitive conditions.[1]

At the heart of this problem is the use of production factors. The scheme for maintaining the equilibrium of one reality is applied to another very different one. It is like mounting a structure on earth using the values of gravity on the moon and the kind of architecture appropriate for Mars. The autonomous power of science and technology overwhelms the power of economies.

Economics burgeoned in the brave new world engendered by the Industrial Revolution, imbued with this same spirit of optimism concerning the power of the human race to control science and technology. But our power suffers from a complex brought on by another power it strives to control. Ever since the Industrial Revolution, economists have simply defined the logic behind the process of scientific and technological development as support elements for ensuring that the economy fulfils its role as swiftly as possible. In doing so, they have basically been united by their unlimited faith in scientific and technological knowledge and their disdain for other forms of knowledge and cultural manifestation. They have been blithely unconcerned about society's cultural enrichment. Economic measurement does not account for production that is not capable of fashioning a commodity. Technology, meanwhile, is reckoned to have unlimited power to produce merchandise.

This creed to which Economics makes its models and theories subscribe is not based on practical observation of the phenomenological world at this point in time nor on projections being made for the coming years. In a way, what happened to the wretched Brazilian scrap-metal merchant and his family in 1987 is what has been happening in the world for the last few decades.

It is obvious that science has granted us an almost complete command of nature. This command has been a positive instrument both with regard to standard economic measurements and in the conquest of greater free time and increasingly sophisticated ways of enjoying it. In recent decades, this advance has generated fascination and generalized optimism regarding technological power. As a result, the whole world is very tolerant of and unperturbed by any risks it may hold for the future. Unlike previous generations, we approach all problems undaunted in the certainty that we can solve them. One instance of this is the current AIDS epidemic which, despite the threat it poses, is tackled with a firm conviction that science will soon devise ways of bringing it under control. Many economists share this feeling when dealing with the risks posed by the economic process. The depletion of resources, pollution, the social distancing of rich and poor are all reckoned to be manifestations of a mutating reality, hurdles that can be 'naturally' overcome thanks to advances in science.

Of late, however, the odds that science will find solutions to economic problems in time to head off high costs give no cause for optimism. It is not a case of imagining an ominous final catastrophe visited upon humankind by the economy. Rather, it is a matter of realizing that such solutions demand more time than is available for warding off high costs. This negative expectation may seem paradoxical at a time when scientific power evolves at break-neck speed. It makes sense, none the less, when one observes that:

(1) Scientific and technological advances have been prodigious not only in providing solutions but also in placing growing demands on the economic system.

(2) These demands have been growing faster than the rate at which discoveries of new natural resources and mechanisms for restoring the ecological balance have advanced.

(3) Scientific discoveries designed to offset risks to the future of the world economy possess ingrained drawbacks, above all when they are not accompanied by social changes adapted to new technological circumstances.

In recent history, if global costs are taken into account, the costs (especially ecological ones) of technological advances have sizeably increased. Traditional mechanisms for occupying forest areas allowed for a degree of ecological balance. Low productivity, demanding great sacrifices in labour for the occupation of each new tract of land, allowed for a degree of interaction between humankind and nature in which neither ever achieved absolute dominion. The use of giant bulldozers and powerful chain-saws has reduced the effort involved in land clearance to such an extent that it now threatens the wholesale destruction of the planet's remaining large forests – unless, that is, it manages to subordinate exploration to a non-economic rationale or to the rationale of another kind of Economics. Nuclear Physics succeeded in mastering matter but generated menacingly perverse effects in the process. If Medicine could suddenly prolong our lives, allowing us say two hundred years of life, we would be plunged into a dire crisis from which we could only extricate ourselves after large-scale wars had wiped out all the benefits obtained thereby – unless, of course, this windfall were combined with a similar surge in food production techniques and a reformulation of political structures.

Blind faith in technological prowess has blotted out awareness of its risks. This is partly because Economics has failed to realize its ubiquity in the web of relations that comprise the ecological system. No attempt has been made to analyse the interaction of technology with life on earth, with the totality of the biosphere, nor with the delicately balanced universe of micro-organisms.[2]

Imbalances are born when technical advance and progress in economic purposes get out of step with the social structure. They would be averted if scientific development was a controllable process and socio-economic structures were to adjust automatically to the requirements of science. This, however, is not how things work.

In recent decades, an apparatus for producing scientific discoveries has been 'scientifically' mounted, in stark contrast to the craft-based *modus operandi* of the 19th and early 20th centuries. Eccentric inventors working in isolation, independently researching the subjects that happen to appeal to them, are already a thing of the past. Most discoveries are now obtained within an industrialized framework of scientific production. The objectives of research are today largely determined by decisions made outside the science community. Research is undertaken by large groups operating on an international scale. Despite this, there is still a good deal of randomness in scientific creation, implying a degree of uncertainty as to the time required to come up with the desired and expected results. Science does still depend for its great leaps forward on the inspiration that strikes the individual researcher in his intellectual solitude, even though such inspiration is often triggered by the stimulus of companionship and debate in select circles of the international scientific community.

This means that discoveries still depend on non-deterministic creativity. There is no way of obtaining hard and fast results to suit a timetable set to meet economic requirements. In cases where a degree of certainty can be had, by dint of the efficiency of big laboratories in meeting requests from their financiers, science is made to toe the line of the economic process, responding to the urge to maximize private profits and not to the desire to solve the major problems of the human race. This is the case in the development of new products – no preventive measures are taken to soften their social and ecological impact. It was the case in the two most important technological projects mounted this century, the Manhattan project for building the first atom bomb, and the Apollo programme to put the first human being on the moon. Even if modern analysis can detect good motives behind the decision to snatch the bomb from Nazi hands and emphasize the universal aspect of the conquest of the moon, it is plain that the motivation was of a national, not a humanitarian nature. The less random scientific creation becomes in order to assume a rationality based on the profit of large corporations or the national interests of superpowers, the less sound or more random the results are from the point of view of humankind.

Marx formulated the idea underpinning historical materialism that technical advance possesses its own dynamics. In its drive to raise profits and compete efficiently in the market, capital is constantly compelled to introduce technical innovations in its equipment. A perfect union between a constant human desire for technical innovation and the specific interests of the economic system is thus celebrated, the knot being tightly tied from the 19th century onwards.

Marx's most important accomplishment was to identify the existence of perpetual tension between technical advance and the social structure. With the evolution of history, the social structure would become an increasingly more serious obstacle to technical advance, and in Marx's opinion this would inexorably ignite the torch of social revolution that would liberate productive forces once more.

Perusing the secular progress of human history, one can perceive a logic in the formulation of this dialectic method that comprises historical materialism. One can hardly be optimistic about applying it to the modern world in the forseeable future, however. Marx miscalculated the pace of technological evolution and underestimated the ability of capitalism to adapt – a phenomenon that only became clearly visible in the 20th century, especially from the 1930s onwards.

Marx failed to predict – and he could hardly have been expected to do so – a new tension between technological advance and the environment. His optimistic outlook led to his viewing capitalism as a system that could only thwart technological advance. He did not envisage it leading instead to the destruction of the environment before a revolutionary process could take shape. This is probably because he never imagined that capitalism would survive so many crises, change shape so as to resume the level of profit-making and impel technological advance into a helter-skelter scramble to develop new products and (as Keynes did) find ways of keeping demand effectively dynamic. Nor could Marx imagine that real socialism would prove incapable of preventing environmental depredation. For him the problem of ecological imbalance simply did not exist. On the contrary, he believed that socialism would unleash society's full potential for consumption and that it would be accessible to all alike without causing alienation. The alienation to which he referred, though, was social alienation between sectors of society. There was as yet no concern that one generation might be alienated from another on account of ecological imbalance. Indeed, Marx held technological prowess to be our *raison d'être*, not a risk, even if collectively owned by an egalitarian but short-sighted society.

Marx failed not in the logic of historical materialism but in mismatching this logic to the dynamics of the real world. This is true, at any rate, within a reasonable time-scale such as the century that has elapsed since the publication of *Das Capital*. His other shortcoming was his failure to associate technological advance, or lack of it, with political progress.

During the 1960s, one of the most important and eminently positive scientific revolutions began to be applied to the benefit of the human race. This consisted of a new method devised by Norman Borlang for the cultivation of wheat and rice, and it was dubbed the 'green revolution'. This discovery provided the world with the prospect of meeting the Asian countries' demand for food staples. Similar techniques have made Brazil one of the world's major cereals exporters. Despite successive agricultural revolutions in recent decades, nutritional penury among the destitute has actually worsened. These revolutions were promoted at the expense of expropriation and concentration of land ownership, leaving peasants jobless and provoking mass migration and a drop in general living standards. Meanwhile, the companies utilizing technological advances grew rich. From the ethical point of view, the green revolution could have been justified if it had lowered food prices and satisfactorily distributed agricultural produce among the entire population both at home and abroad. This was not the case. Food prices continued to be dictated by international speculation and demand remained concentrated in the hands of a minority with the power to purchase the produce. The idea that supply would generate its own demand overlooked the fact that demand is moulded to the distribution of income. Far from improving the level of food consumption among the undernourished, the increase in Brazil's agricultural production has been used to raise the quality of foodstuffs consumed in rich countries, soya being exported as fodder for European cattle.

This would still leave open the possibility that these exports were providing Brazil with foreign currency earnings, enabling it to purchase abroad the foodstuffs required to feed its undernourished population. This has not and does not occur for two reasons. First, because in present circumstances all Brazil's foreign currency earnings are barely sufficient to pay the interest on its external debt and thus do not enable the country to import foreign commodities. Secondly, because, even if this stumbling block did not exist, the free market and income concentration in Brazil would ensure that such imports were channelled away from providing food for the poor. Brazil could import to satisfy either the direct demand of the rich or in order to undertake industrial investments aimed at meeting effective demand originating in the wealthy sector of the population.

The problem stems from a social structure in which land ownership and mercantile production combine to form a rationale that posits nourishment as a means of boosting profits and global capital accumulation rather than as a goal in itself. Owing to the structure and conception of the economy, the green revolution – like all scientific inventions – ends up as an instrument for fuelling the dynamism of the economic process instead of contributing to extend freedom by means of the economic process.[3] More critical still is the matter of agricultural pesticides: rather than solving the problem of undernourishment, much agricultural produce surreptitiously poisons the population that consumes it.

If a discovery with such obviously positive possibilities has failed to deliver the desired results, generating unemployment and impoverishment among the masses, similarly daunting results must surely be expected from scientific innovations in fashionable, leading-edge fields such as biotechnology, microelectronics, computer technology and the like.

Scientists tend to put the blame for the negative side-effects of their discoveries on the politicians and social scientists who, at the end of the 20th century, continue to reason on the basis of the same principles (and some even more backward) that Plato was defending 2,500 years ago. To right this state of affairs, instead of putting forward a revolution in the relation of science to society, reorganising the latter in order to adapt it to the possibilities of modern knowledge, many scientists clamour for absolute individual freedom. They forget that this freedom is false, since their work is a response to questions posed within the rational framework of a backward economic system. Even if a scientist could actually work freely, like some latter-day white-coated Robinson Crusoe, his brainchildren would not be transformed into real effects if they did not dance to the tune of the economic system. They also forget that the consequences of the use made of their discoveries have an increasingly socialized impact, while the determination of their use is still wholly captive to private interests. The decision to build a supertanker to transport several million tons of oil is taken by a small group of company directors and is normally designed to increase the profits of its future owners. The engineering project itself is governed by the imperative of boosting the company's profits and is entrusted to a small management group; the route the ship is to sail is determined by economies in fuel consumption and the captain's skill in keeping costs to a minimum. The consequences of transporting such vast quantities of oil, however, may benefit or harm millions or even billions of people.

The same applies to any other action ensuing from great technical advances in the fields of nuclear technology, applied biology, etc. The impact of such actions is becoming increasingly widespread, but their perpetrators continue to act alone or in small groups. The world has witnessed a constant extension of the risks it faces from science and technology, while the costs and benefits they bring have not been correspondingly shared out.

By laying bare the contradiction between the social mechanism of production and private ownership of the means of production, Marx forecast such consequences in detail where the economic process is concerned. The time was not yet ripe for predicting such effects on a planetary scale. There will be precious little time, however, for us to reach an understanding on the matter and settle on a line of action to avoid enormous continuing, even irreversible, costs.

Sadly, a number of physicists who have examined the subject propose that social concerns be made subordinate to scientific interests rather than, on the contrary, accepting that technological advance should be governed by the ethics of a different human society. Instead of pressing science and technology into the service of a quest to broaden the horizon of freedom of the human race, they intend to stifle this freedom in order to reduce the risks of misuse of their discoveries. This social adaptation, which many scientists (some in a veiled fashion) embrace, would produce a definitive about-turn from the desire that science be put to good use by society. Indeed, this attitude positively fosters the ill use of society by science. Karl Popper, who was devoted to the social study of science, expressed a prejudice against scientists, of whom he said: 'Physicists, with a few brilliant exceptions, have remained aloof from all these philosophical debates.'[4] Brian Easlea, who abandoned a brilliant career as a nuclear physicist in order to concentrate on studying philosophy and the sociology of science, has levelled strong criticism at the role of scientists in the modern world. He demonstrated the logical complicity between the neutral desire to pursue science and the military strategy for winning the war.[5] The relationship between physical and social scientists, especially economists, is no different, the same applying to the relationship between economists and the military and politicians in dictatorial régimes, particularly in the Third World.

The solution is not to put the brake on discoveries and limit the uses of scientific potential. Nor is it a matter of handing science a *carte blanche*. Rather, we should make science the basic instrument for achieving freedom for society and for each individual. Science should be allowed to roam free in its quest for knowledge, but it must be controlled by society when it serves to trample on rather than promote freedom, be it in the present or the future. For this to come about, we need regulatory ethics to govern the role and uses of science and technology. Such ethics must subordinate them to the building of freedom, drawing on the efficiency with which the economy produces goods and services. The new ethics must be grounded in the practice of freedom represented by the pure knowledge of science, as well as by the arts and philosophical reflection.[6]

Notes

1. For further details, see *Tecnologia Apropriada: Una Política para la Banca de Desarrollo* by C. Buarque & S.C. Buarque, Lima, ALIDE, 1983, pp. 14-18.

2. One can even claim that plagues have played a positive role in maintaining the balance in areas overpopulated by human beings, producing healthier, more resistant growth in the surviving population. William H. McNeill's *Plagues and Peoples* (New York, Anchor Books, 1976) explores the integration between human organisms and bacteria, microbes and other parasites that have inflicted plagues on human societies. He also examines the historical consequences of plagues for humankind as a whole and for a number of specific groups. He considers, for instance, the conquest of Mexico in which the smallpox virus was Cortez's staunchest soldier against Montezuma. This is indirectly confirmed by the Aztec account of the invasion published as *The Broken Spear: The Aztec Account of the Conquest of Mexico*, edited by Miguel Leon Portilla, Boston, Beacon Press, 1962.

3. There are numerous books on this subject. See, particularly, F.M. Lappé & J. Collins, *Food First: Beyond the Myth of Scarcity*, New York, Ballantine Books, 1977, and Susan George, *How the Other Half Dies*, New Jersey, Allanheld, Osmun & Co., 1977.

4. Karl Popper, *Conjectures and Refutations: The Growth of Scientific Knowledge*, New York, Harper & Row, 1968, p. 99.

5. His *Liberation and the Aims of Science* (London, Chatto & Windus, 1973), which bears the subtitle 'An essay on the obstacles to building a more beautiful world', is a manifesto against science being used by groups in power and against society being used by science. In Brazil, Regina Lucia de Moraes Morel analyses one aspect of the problem in *Ciência e Estado: A Política Científica no Brasil* <Science and state: science policy in Brazil>, São Paulo, Ed. Toco, 1979. For a broader approach, see Bertrand Russell's *The Impact of Science on Society*, New York, Simon & Schuster, 1953.

6. See C. Buarque, *Na Fronteira do Futuro* (At the frontier of the future), Brasília, Brasília University Press, 1989.

CHAPTER 7

The Value of Nature

The environment and the economy

In any biological species, each individual's survival depends on direct symbiosis with nature through the intake of nourishment.

Human beings, however, have differed from other species since the most primitive stages of their development. The first difference is that instead of symbiotically appropriating nature, humans use intermediary elements in the form of tools. Things cease to be consumed in the shape in which they are encountered in nature, and become differentiated by-products of human labour. Goods thus arise as non-natural elements of nature. The second difference is that by dint of their use of these tools and as a result of social co-operation between individuals, humans have succeeded in reducing the time required for the struggle to survive. They have thus conquered free time for the exercise of cultural activities and the development of new tools for achieving greater efficiency and conquering even more free time. It is on account of this feature of the human process that the ecological dilemma has arisen. The trouble is that humankind sees itself and its artefacts as separate from the rest of nature.

Nature maintains a continuous cycle of life in balance through regulatory mechanisms that control the interaction of species. If one species reproduces excessively, sources of food for it will become scarce and demographic growth will automatically slow down.

This view of nature, along with the observation that natural elements are integrated in and subject to a global logic, led to the earth being conceived of as a giant living organism. This organism, of which the human species is but a tiny part, was baptized 'Gaia' (after the Greek goddess of the earth). Consigned to oblivion after its first consideration by the Scottish geologist James Hutton, the sentiment and concept of the earth (and the life it sustains) as a unitary element began to gain acceptance in the 1980s with the constant reformulation and improvement of the idea launched by James Lovelock and Lynn Marguilis. Initially it met with considerable incredulity. The ingrained view of life as an individual manifestation of each species and each separate being, and the position of the human race at the hub of the universe, representing an omnipotent God, had made the hypothesis of a global organism encompassing all forms of life on the planet a mere mental exercise. Modifications to the original presentation of the idea, the availability of instruments for analysing the global interrelations between species and between environments, and knowledge of the intimate details of life – all these have helped to spread acceptance of the idea of Gaia among the scientific community.

At the same time, the increasing perturbations that the economic process inflicts on the balance in which Gaia exists and evolves are becoming more obvious. First, because Economics is charged with the notion of history, urging the need for the predominance of one species. Instead of viewing history as an unconscious natural phenomenon consisting of long cycles in which species compete and succeed each other, human beings saw themselves as the culmination of the evolutionary process, and necessary, therefore, for justifying nature. Secondly, because history has recently come to be seen as part of a linear process of progress, marked by the pace at which natural raw materials are transformed into economic goods. Thirdly, because this process is accelerating so fast that nature has no chance of restoring the balance. This seriously jeopardizes not only the balance of nature but also our prospects of survival after many other species have been driven to extinction by the undiscriminating scythe of economic transformation. For the first time, an imbalance of the global living organism, leading to the extinction of species, springs from the direct interference of one particular species. Even recent theories about the part life may have played in controlling the earth's climate are based on the effects of the sum total of life on the biosphere, the quantity of oxygen, heat absorption, and so on.

It was the dimension of economic growth that first upset the balance. The use of human intelligence in creating instruments to master nature has apparently led to what the Chilean economist Max Neef calls the manifestation of the only stupid species in the universe. By the might of its lesser but logical intelligence, the human race was destroying a greater, though non-logical, intelligence. Or, to put it another way, by the logic of their system, human beings were destroying a greater intelligence manifested in the balance of nature. The perverse, unintelligent spin-offs of the economic process can be observed in its twin effects: depredation of resources, leading to extinction and depletion; and environmental pollution, which fosters further extinction.

The depredation of resources

Natural resources must be understood historically from the point of view of the technological standards obtaining at any particular time. The slice of nature classified as natural resources changes with the passage of time, both through the incorporation of new substances and by the obsolescence of others. Until a hundred years ago, crude oil was not a natural resource; nor was uranium until a few decades ago. From the economic standpoint, the concept of nature is equally susceptible to time, the economy's sole interest residing in that portion of it that contains resources. On the other hand, only those elements which, besides being raw materials for some technological process, can be restricted and controlled by ownership, can be considered resources.

Without rejecting the premises of technological necessity and ownership of scarce resources, modern economists have added the concept of the economic value of such resources, based not only on their market price but also on the impact that scarcity has on the population's consumption of the resource. They have advanced by attempting to venture beyond the market as an all-determining factor, but have made paltry progress in attributing value to nature itself. They have made allowance for scarcity but have assumed that it will somehow be overcome.

Ecological impact on natural resources may spark off a reduction in consumption due to the impossibility of continuing a particular activity, or on account of soaring production costs. In both cases, this impact does not depend solely on natural factors, such as the size of reserves or the natural renewability of the resources involved. It is also dependent upon technological features, including the recycling of products and the substitution of resources.

(1) Natural impact: the bigger the reserves, the smaller the economic impact of the destruction of part of the resource; negative impact will likewise diminish proportionally as the probability of encountering new reserves increases; finally, this impact subsides and may disappear if nature itself renews the special types of renewable resource.

(2) The impact of technological innovation: due to modern recycling methods, the resource employed may be re-used, thus postponing depletion of its reserves; technological innovation may also provide for the substitution of resources that are becoming scarce, making them obsolete and so reducing ecological impact to negligible levels from the economic standpoint.

Apart from these natural and technological factors, the economic costs of ecological impacts on reserves of natural resources can be altered by means of social changes, especially in terms of consumption levels suited to the civilizational model. The most important example of the searing effect of the depredation of a natural resource in the modern world is the consumption of oil. This situation can be righted by raising known reserves, although exploring them would tend to be increasingly expensive; by making use of renewable fuels such as alcohol and alternative plant or hydro-electric energy sources; by developing more efficient motors and recovering residues currently discarded; and by creating new technologies for tapping hitherto unknown reserves, and for extraction at depths and in locations that are presently unprofitable from an economic standpoint. However, the most efficient solution – though perhaps not the easiest or most profitable one – is to reduce consumption, as opposed to frantically searching for alternative sources.

Modern consumer society, particularly in the Third World, influenced by the North American view of progress, has created the myth of a correlation between the level of well-being and *per capita* income, and between *per capita* income and *per capita* consumption of fuel oil. The facts show that this correlation is not in the least linear. Comparison of European societies with society in the United States demonstrates that social democracy, and even real socialism in Eastern Europe, have been capable of creating a higher standard of living than one might expect given their *per capita* incomes. This is a result of income distribution and social investment. More importantly, examination of the oil consumption/*per capita* income ratio shows that Europeans, with much better welfare standards than Americans, consume less oil *per capita* because of their different transport systems and alternative energy generation schemes.

There is no sign that this alternative to the North American energy model is inferior from the point of view of well-being. Trains and buses running to schedule on electric energy over a great variety of routes, with sufficient seating capacity and temperature control in regions affected by intense cold or heat, probably provide a higher standard of social welfare than do private vehicles. Providing, that is, that one pays no heed to the status that consumer society, by means of advertisements, holds out to the prospective owners of modern vehicles, designed to cruise like racing cars. In their humdrum, everyday life, however, motorists are ensnared by traffic jams in big cities, their fine automobiles turned to golden prisons specially designed for burning up fossil fuels.

Protection of scarce resources can best be achieved (and with a greater chance of success) by a reduction in *per capita* consumption brought about by a change in society's energy system, rather than relying on the off-chance of locating new reserves or stumbling on new technologies.

Pollution

The production system transforms natural resources into goods that are later dumped on nature. Besides the depredation of the resources it employs, the production process creates three types of pollution:

(1) A basically social impact, like the stench of a distillery, the noise in neighbourhoods located near airport runways, or air and water made unfit for leisure purposes.

(2) A basically economic impact, by which the production process aggravates the depletion of resources, destroying them both in the short term (e.g. by reducing fish reserves) and in the long term (e.g. through desertification).

(3) A basically biological impact, causing a drop in public health standards, the emergence of new diseases, or the destruction of entire species, such as occurs in the reservoirs formed by hydro-electric schemes or in urban centres that grow up around industrial parks, especially those with a concentration of chemical and petrochemical industries.

Economics has been analysing the problem of how to measure the ecological impact of pollution on the basis of this systematic approach. Cost-benefit ratios have led to the development of methods capable of quantifying ecological impacts. But the technical foundations of cost-benefit ratios limit considerations to an economic figure system, international currencies or the aggregate value of the consumption generated or destroyed.[1] These methods fail to incorporate all the consequences of the impact production has on nature.

Most economists are still blinkered by the optimistic view of industrial production that has prevailed since the end of the 18th century. They overlook the global scope of impacts and eschew long-term analysis. This is why ecological impact has been held to be unrelated to economic matters as traditionally conceived. What has interested economists is the effect on prices of the shrinking supply of a resource or the impurity of the air and water in major cities, or even the greater risk of planetary desertification. In a number of cases, such as natural landscapes, forestry and wildlife reserves, the value and cost of depletion and extinction have been assessed purely in terms of their impact on tourist activities and other forms of recreation.

Economic reductionism of this kind has its own logic. The value of nature as such has been the concern of physicists and philosophers, not of economists. For the latter, the definition of natural value is a strictly technological and legal matter. That is why the science of Economics had no reason for and no means of including the environment in its analytical framework.

The situation today is entirely different. The availability of previously abundant resources in the public domain is under threat. A feeling, not yet incorporated into the simplistic analysis of tangible exchange values, is beginning to take shape: that the habitat in which the drama of civilization is played out demands special attention. There is a new-found need to incorporate value into the intangible heritage that the environment represents for our culture as the basis of the biological process, regardless of its productive repercussions in the economy.

We therefore need to adapt the principles of economic analysis to the designs and logic of a civilization in ecological balance with the environment that sustains it – an environment that constitutes the heritage that the process of civilization seeks to enhance.

Optimism in economic theory

From a purely economic standpoint, incorporating ecological impact into the production system implies quantifying it – as a negative or positive datum – in the value of the goods obtained. The limitations of economic theory have made this incorporation impossible both with regard to the conception of value and as far as the time horizon is concerned. All economic schools are loath to acknowledge that nature has a value in itself. All have proved impotent to administer the long term in which the results of ecological impact are most clearly felt.

According to neo-classical theory, the price of manufactures depends exclusively on a balance between supply and demand for goods, whether they be the end-products that consumers buy on the retail market, or inputs purchased by manufacturers. To be measured, ecological impact will have to be part of the prevailing consumer psychology. It is the consumer's sentiment that would then determine the ecological balance. It is impossible to obtain a natural balance based on the impossible reconciliation of the individual's short-term choice with society's long-term historical preoccupations. Besides, the balance between supply and demand is based on the prices demanded by economic agents and fails to make sense when applied to public assets such as the air or a forest. The individual consumer's interest and rationale are naturally short-sighted. Under the influence of neo-classical theory, society would adopt a generalized ecological option only if the imbalance of nature were so immediate as to make it too late to avert its consequences.

Even now that there are clear signs of a drastic reduction in the ozone layer, of the fouling of the atmosphere in big cities, and of the risk of a real shortage of certain resources, the ecological question is still being debated. Decisions are now being taken by political leaders motivated by ideological, ethically defined concerns. Owing to the burgeoning awareness of ecological risks, one can now expect the population of Europe to vote for protective measures banning the use of certain pollutants. One would have to be blind to the difference between the political psychology of the masses and the psychological urge of each individual to consume to expect there to be a general, spontaneous move to abstain from consuming such products.

On the grounds of this selfsame analysis, businessmen (including the executives of state-owned companies) cannot, in their drive to boost profits, make allowance for the very long-term prospect of real scarcity, much less the future costs of pollution. Even so, one can detect ecological awareness spreading faster in the business community than among economists. Entrepreneurial think-tanks are appearing all over the world, and business concerns are searching for alternative manufacturing processes. This is more the fruit of a global preoccupation with the world and scarcity than the upshot of partial solutions in each individual company.

Classical theory incorporates a basic premise which philosophically prevents the concept of exhaustibility being included in its schemes: the view that egoistic utilitarianism is the bedrock of the economic rationale. The acceptance of this rationale – of maximizing social welfare through individual interests – makes it impossible to consider long-term and medium-term exhaustibility since individual preferences take account only of the short term and of the individual's immediate surroundings. There is no reason to include the extinction of a species, the depletion of a resource or environmental pollution in a business's flow of funds or in an individual's consumer preferences.

Economists prefer to maintain the idea of limitless replaceability in their theoretical schema as a form of defence. According to this view, real exhaustibility does not correspond to economic exhaustibility since economic agents sense the change in relative prices, raising the price of products that are becoming scarce by investing and finding other cheaper substitutes. This idea of elastic substitution masks the reality of exhaustibility and creates the illusion of a smooth road to inexhaustibility. This view implicitly assumes that technological advance has the power to create whatever it pleases, taking the time it pleases. Not the least account is taken of the negative effects of its creation.

The Marxist notion of value does not make full allowance for either the exhaustibility of resources or the cost of pollution. Although he does not transfer the essence of value to the realm of individual psychology, for Marx, as for the classical theorists who preceded him, the value of things is determined solely by the quantity of labour they contain. Besides, the Marxist view of history is radically optimistic about the potential of technological advance. Marxists see this as boundless (providing the obstacles of social structures are overcome), and as a determining factor of social progress itself.

Marx forecast the trend towards diminishing global profits in the capitalist economy, but for reasons very different from the depredation of the environment. As he saw it, the slump would be brought about by what he termed the organic composition of capital which, as a result of competition between businesses, makes for growing capitalization through the use of novel manufacturing techniques and new machinery. But Marx was as full of optimism as the neo-classicists and even more so than classical theorists. He predicted that dwindling profits, instead of generating a stagnant economy, would spell the downfall of capitalism. Structural modifications in society would enable socialism and communism to confer on the human race unlimited abundance and free time.

From the Marxist standpoint, temporary exhaustibility signifies an increase in the quantity of labour required to obtain a resource or product. The reaction to this would be to find substitutes for each resource whenever its exhaustion begins to demand more labour in order to obtain or produce it. Alternatively, modifications in the social structure would come about so as to liberate the creative energy to forge technological innovation. Whatever the case, exhaustibility would subside without leaving social scars. This stance can be deemed even less ecological if one considers that, by cutting back on the quantity of labour through technological innovation, one may be enhancing the depredation of nature, however much real exhaustibility and scarcity there may be.

The last century and a half have demonstrated to neo-classical and Marxist analysts alike that exhaustibility is an unjustifiably pessimistic concept. Technological advance over this period has grafted into people's minds a belief in the inexhaustibility of resources, due to the boundless human capacity for innovation. This fosters a relentless surge in productivity while also encouraging the discovery of new resources. Agriculture, which David Ricardo put forward as a prime example for his theory of diminishing returns, in fact proved the opposite. Instead of a rapid exhaustion of fertile lands (which Malthus predicted would spread wide-scale famine, and Ricardo estimated would produce a zero yield, capable of ensuring no more than the physical survival of those cultivating them), what we have witnessed is the growing potential of lands previously held to be unsuitable for cultivation. The immediate future may also give rise to optimism, especially if one discounts the toxic side-effects of many modern fertilizers.

The rejection of Ricardo's and especially Malthus's predictions led to an outright dismissal of the pessimism that pervaded part of the 19th century with regard to the availability of natural resources. Since then economists have been the very picture of optimism. The only bone of contention has been the divide between neo-classicists, who have extolled the infinite possibilities of capitalism, and Marxists, who have upheld the boundless potential of socialism once alienation and exploitation have been expunged.

Neither school sensed any need to include the environmental dimension in their analyses. The neo-classicists' market and the Marxists' social revolutions would unleash the technological forces needed to avert any risk of exhaustion of natural resources.

The events of the last few decades, however, indicate that optimistic analyses are insufficient to mould a rational approach to the future. Ecological costs are more than simple economic statistics, and there is no way of incorporating them by methods designed to maximize the profits of each economic agent. In other words, they have no place in neo-classical analyses, and Marxist ideology falls short of the mark.

The discovery of the environment

The disparity between the minute size of human economic output and the apparently infinite availability of the planet's natural resources was one of the reasons for the optimism that prevailed until the 1960s. This does not, however, explain Western society's disdain for nature, which was clear even before industrialization. Observation of the behaviour of primitive societies blessed with abundant resources – as in the case of Indian tribes in the West of the United States, for instance – reveals that this attitude has more to do with the philosophical underpinnings of anthropocentrism than with a particular economic environment. Only a few thinkers in the West (including Rousseau, St Francis of Assisi and Emerson) have framed a view of nature distinct from both the scientist's itch to probe and master its secrets without ever respecting it as an animate being and the poet's response to it as a source of pure yet soulless beauty.

Ecological concern thus begins to seep into Western attitudes not as a result of the discovery of nature but because the risk of its destruction is finally perceived. The distinguishing feature of 'neo-Malthusians' is their rational awareness of the 'limits to economic growth', encapsulated in the title of the Club of Rome Report. This is a milestone in the prolific literature which, since the end of the 1960s, has sent up a cry of warning, denouncing the imminent risk of ecological imbalance. It is this awakening of conscience, indeed, that has led to Western culture's discovery of nature.

The Report was not born of the concern of economists, however. Quite the opposite. Many of them, however, reacted to its conclusions, especially to its recommendations for a general slow-down in economic growth across the globe. A letter from Sicco Mansholt to the president of the European Economic Community in February 1972, in which (as a member of the EEC's Executive Committee) he raised questions about the significance and consequences of economic growth, thrust the issue into the limelight.[2] It was Third World economists, even the most critical of them, fired with enthusiasm for the vigorous growth of the 1960s and early 1970s, that put up the most vociferous barrage of opposition.

Members of the Third World's technocracy, returning from the USA with their hard-won neo-classical baggage to play the spoilt boys of their countries' dictatorships, with entire countries at their disposal as veritable laboratories for their fiendish experiments and solid credit in international banks for financing their projects, could hardly be expected to surrender to pessimism. More critical economists, of Marxist lineage or advocates of ECLA-style developmentalism, also kept the flame of optimism burning. They favoured the same sort of growth that the technocrats propounded, provided that the dictatorship was dispensed with and social justice was promoted through an income distribution policy. They cultivated the same disdain for the environmental dimension – to their minds, a distracting ploy trumped up by imperialism and the hippies.

Criticism of the Club of Rome's conclusion was harshest among economists who inveighed against capitalist growth, especially Marxists. A counter-current burgeoned among left-wing economists in the Third World. They argued that the neo-Malthusian outlook and concern about the environment were part of an orchestrated strategy for preventing the advancement and economic independence of developing countries. Criticism was still levelled at poor income distribution and not at the global perversity of growth models that required the concentration of wealth.

The few economists who at that point had the foresight to grasp the global dimensions of the ecological conundrum amid this spate of optimism deserve special mention. Ignacy Sachs examined the issue at length. His seminars at the École Pratique des Hautes Études Sociales in Paris in the early 1970s influenced an entire generation of economists.[3] Many then heard the word ecology spoken for the first time as something that made sense.

Special mention should also be made of Josué de Castro who, as early as the 1940s in Brazil, criticized the way economic growth related to nature. De Castro was probably the first person to put forward the choice between 'steel and bread' as a dilemma. Until then, everyone took it for granted that 'bread' (meaning food and welfare) depended on 'steel' (meaning industrialization).[4] In the United States, Georgescu-Roegen was not only a pioneer but also one of the finest analysts of the relations between Economics, the concept of entropy, and the economic process.

Although it continued to be a theoretical taboo among economists, the subject was studied by analysts from different backgrounds. The MIT group, coordinated by Dennis and Donella Meadows,[5] elaborated the systemic model and processed the data that the Club of Rome (under the leadership of Aurelio Peccei[6]) had requested for formulating the conclusions published in 1968. A small but significant study by a renowned English intellectual and politician, E.F. Schumacher, also drew attention to the issue.[7]

Until then, only naturalists and the hippie movement had voiced concern about nature. In the wake of these pioneering studies, concern about the state of the world and the intellectual desire to keep abreast of the issues of the day led to a proliferation of studies. The Stockholm Conference on the Environment, held in 1972, was decisive for publicizing the state of the environment and its relation to Economics. At the same time, criticism of Western rationalism burgeoned. Alternative proposals for viewing the world based on oriental thinking and existentialism were put forth, mainly by Allan Watts,[8] Theodore Rozzak[9] and, at a later date, Fritjof Capra. But only in the 1980s can we find a real analytical endeavour to combine Economics, Ethics and Ecology of the kind that Herman Daly and John B. Cobb have been making.[10]

Were it indeed the fad many imagined it to be, or were it merely some devious stratagem of American imperialism, as many Third World economists believed, the issue would certainly not have remained centre-stage. A real neo-Malthusian movement in all its colours was only able to attain global scope, as we can see it now, due to novel circumstances that brought together four levels of awareness and knowledge:

(1) The technical level. Three new, hitherto non-existent analytical instruments became available. To begin with, the theories and tools of systemic analysis made it possible to mount global models of the world, interrelating multifarious economic variables involving both production and consumption while also assessing their impacts. Secondly, statistical data made it possible to quantify relations and define technical coefficients. Such data enabled analysts to gauge trends in output and consumption, the demands they placed on resources and the wastes they generated. Finally, large-scale data-processing techniques and equipment were developed, without which these systems and data would not have been dynamic enough for analysis.

(2) The level of collective awareness. Awareness of ecological disasters has increased greatly since the Minamata affair, manifest in the filthy air of big cities, in the grimy rivers of Europe and, soon afterwards, in nuclear accidents and the burning of the rainforests. This awareness made it evident that the soaring level of output and consumption, compounded by the wastage of modern society, was leading to dramatic depredation of resources and producing dangerously high levels of pollution.

(3) The political level. OPEC, the petroleum cartel, took advantage of the 1973 Middle East War to introduce what, from the economic standpoint, was a sudden, 'artificial' and 'arbitrary' rise in the price of crude oil. Despite the pretext of war, the argument they used to justify this move was that petroleum reserves would soon run dry. They certainly had recourse to the conclusions of the Club of Rome in order to bring home the fact that each country's resources were not perennial. The solution, they claimed, was to raise oil prices so as to obtain swifter returns or to spin out their assets. OPEC could not have adopted this stance had it not been for the spread of anti-colonialist sentiments. These had been fermenting since the Second World War and had found in the Vietnam War an example of how colonized peoples could resist the onslaught when imbued with firm determination.[11]

(4) The ideological level. There is no denying that the hippie protest movement has weighed upon the world's collective consciousness. An offshoot of existentialism and descendant of the beatnik movements that had long been berating consumer society, the hippie

movement and the malaise of the Vietnam War dominated the second half of the 1960s and a good deal of the 1970s. One cannot turn a blind eye to the fact that this criticism, taken to the extremes of 1968 throughout the world, undermined the foundations of consumer ideology. It rattled the theoretical mainstays of the traditional left wing, challenging existing orthodoxies, and allowed consumer elites in the First World to adopt a critical approach to the societies being built there.

The difficulties of incorporating nature into Economics

What the Club of Rome and subsequent economic analysis did was to demonstrate, by means of statistical projections, the extreme unlikelihood that the pace of growth attained in recent years could be sustained.[12] Although this and other studies have succeeded in denouncing the ecological consequences of the economic process, they do not fathom its essence. They do not come to grips with a logic that would enable one to influence the management of the process. With rare exceptions, these studies are basically statistical projections of current trends that assume, *ceteris paribus*, that present consumer demands and technical coefficients will continue to behave in much the same way. At most, they undertake sensitivity surveys as a means of defining different possible scenarios.

Such superficial models are a direct result of the limitations of Economics. It is a science that does not possess the analytical instruments for definitively and effectively incorporating the real trend of the economy. Nine limiting factors stand in the way of this incorporation.

Demographic growth

Some neo-Malthusians consider demographic growth to be one of the main sources of impact on the environment. Population growth does indeed place greater demands on resources and may provoke environmental pollution. Demographic growth increases needs, compelling the productive sector to churn out its goods at such a rate that it fiercely fuels the demand for resources. These much-wanted resources in turn tend to entail growing production costs, forcing up prices.

It is, however, a distortion to believe that this is the determining factor. The population affects the environment according to the prevailing socio-economic system. Populations as distinct as those of the Third World and those of Western Europe and the United States or, within the Third World, countries such as Brazil, China or India, all produce different impacts on the environment.

On the other hand, from this traditional slant, warped by traditional economic attitudes, population is viewed as a means and not as the objective of the civilization process. More attention is paid to each individual's material consumption than to the global (especially cultural) value of the world's population.

Socio-economic articulation

Almost all neo-Malthusian economists who have made projections for the future assume that a catastrophic trend is inevitable unless the pace of economic growth slows down. This is the gist of the Club of Rome's opening proposal, which recommends deliberate stifling of the growth rate (zero growth) as a means of averting disaster.

This proposal is in turn based on a mechanistic metaphysical conception which envisages the problem as a purely economic quandary stemming from production, while seeing its underlying social structure and purpose as unchanging data. It leads one to view environmental impact as a problem caused by the supply generated by the economy and not as a spin-off of the quantitative and qualitative demand exerted by society on the production system. Finally, it ignores the fact that ecological impact is in many cases wrought more directly by social features than by physical effects.

The fact is that environmental impact is a direct consequence of each specific socio-economic framework. Every little ripple in each sector of this framework contaminates contiguous sectors, triggering further effects in a complex web of articulations involving society and the environment. This web involves consumer standards, urban infrastructure, cultural values, the level of technical innovation, and so on.

Of all the vectors that make up the web of environmental impacts, the most directly important is the model of production, associated with consumption standards. This explains why it is the standard of consumption that determines the level of harm done to the environment. The automobile is the most visible emblem of a broader system now described as consumerism. The basic character of modern capitalist society is necessarily predatory and polluting due to two factors: it demands constantly expanding output and a persistent endeavour to cut production costs.

Other than in short periods during technological revolutions, increased output implies increased depredation of nature. The drive to slash production costs heightens the impact of depredation as a result of the necessary cut-back in investments for obtaining alternative materials, regenerative equipment, etc.

Only legal measures can reverse the depredation trend. With very few exceptions, these measures are un- or even anti-economic. One exception is when depredation has been so devastating that it generates employment and income through ecological clean-up industries.

The impact of the economic process on the environment thus depends on the model of civilization in which it is encapsulated. The problem cannot be addressed without taking stock of the entire web of socio-economic relations. On the other hand, the idea of zero growth on a global scale overlooks the political and ethical unfeasibility of freezing (and therefore perpetuating) the present, unequal level of consumption between nations.

The technological apparatus

Each technology possesses its own characteristic pollutants and depredatory traits. As it is the technological paradigm that defines consumption patterns in the modern world, the problem of technological options lies at the heart of the ecological dilemma.

Though the level of technology actually present in the economy is determined by the prevailing socio-economic system, one can view the specific, increasingly autonomous technology sub-sector as having its own effects on the environment. This means that one can pursue a model of civilization with diverse technological schemes and differing patterns of consumption.

The problem is, once again, compounded in the case of societies importing technology from more developed nations. When transplanted, these technologies bring with them all their polluting, depredatory components with two aggravating features. The first is that technological backwardness and the paucity of funds prevent the development of techniques for combatting pollution and researching alternative resources. Secondly, these techniques have been designed to operate with natural resources available in other environments, thus obliging already poor countries to import the resources now required. This fosters another form of depredation through dependence which, in the scramble to generate foreign currency earnings, depredates local natural resources as well as exploiting human labour.

The problem of pricing and real scarcity

The difficulties involved in making reliable projections of the effects of technological progress in replacing natural resources and of achieving precise estimates of the real availability of these resources in nature makes it impossible to fix correct future prices.

Petroleum is one instance of this problem. Of all the basic inputs on which our present civilization relies, oil is the one whose geological location is best known. It is, moreover, one of the resources most likely to run out in the short term. None the less, it would be a rash gamble to fix a future price for oil on the basis of the real scarcity that lurks just a few decades ahead, for one cannot be certain that it will not have been substituted by another cheaper, more efficient fuel.

Such impotence with regard to the future amounts to methodological suicide for the present science of Economics, for it is incapable of predicting and formulating alternative forms of measurement that reflect real costs. It would equally be its demise as an instrument of social organization.

Even if they acknowledge the risk and probability of imprecise price estimates in an economy gripped by predictable, real scarcity, responsible economists must formulate alternatives that can at least serve as guidelines for decision-makers.

A proposal for instruments to incorporate real scarcity into the estimation of future prices has been made in a text published by the Economics Department at Brasília University in 1979.[13] It consists in the use of a relative exhaustibility factor for correcting economic or social prices, adjusting them so as to take account of real scarcity. For each resource, this factor would be calculated by a formula that takes into account the forecast period of time that will elapse before the resource is exhausted, and incorporates an elasticity indicating the replaceability of one resource by another. By using prices corrected by an exhaustibility factor, one would be able to gauge a project's effect on nature from the point of view of resources. Each project could then be rated by its entropic effect, based on the ratio between the rate of return calculated using prices corrected by the exhaustibility factor and the rate of return calculated at normal economic prices.

The problem of intangible impact

Much of a project's impact, especially the extent to which it may destroy parts of the physical environment that are without economic value, is intangible, making it impossible to evaluate in quantitative terms. This is true of the extinction of animal species, the destruction of archaeological monuments, the suffering caused by the ailments fostered by economic progress, and so on. The economic analyst must account for such impacts. Modern economists, however, are convinced that it is scientifically impossible to take into account anything that cannot be quantified. Given the choice between the acuity of an analysis that incorporates real but intangible considerations and the methodological elegance of eschewing subjective considerations, economists prefer to shun reality for the sake of methodology.

There is a wealth of literature on this subject, including proposals that attempt to quantify 'goods' such as life, archaeological heritage and so on in terms of their impact on gross product.[14] However, they all try to complement Economics from outside its theoretical framework, when the ideal approach would be to formulate instruments that would enable one to analyse such impact by means of economic analysis *per se*. This is unlikely to be possible since much of this impact depends on value judgements. Yet scientific purity (viewed from an angle other than the influence Newtonian Physics has exerted on economists) would not be marred were Economics itself to be capable of absorbing value judgements by incorporating ethical principles into its theoretical framework.

The national outlook

The science of Economics emerged, in Adam Smith's works, as a cosmopolitan, intellectual approach designed to counter mercantilist protectionism. It defines a country's wealth by its productive potential, its dynamics being dictated by free trade and not by the amassing of treasure. Despite this, all economic accounting is applied to nations or smaller accounting units such as states, boroughs, companies or individuals. In no case does accounting enlarge its scope to include greater units such as a group of nations. Ever since Adam Smith, economists have taken cosmopolitan stands on economic relations but have remained provincial inasmuch as they restrict measurement of the effects of these relations and other aspects of productive activity to national units.

Though it may be correct to plump for nations as the ideal units for analysing social welfare, this focus fails to register the polluting effects of projects whose impacts span frontiers, much less of those that attain a planetary scale. Nowadays, projects have growing international impacts, though many may leave only slight or even no traces of pollution within the frontiers of the countries in which they operate. Even though it fails to make a clean break with the national outlook in economic measurement, a study entitled *Assessment of Multinational Projects*[15] does attempt to gauge the international impact of national projects. It uses a methodology in which each project should also be analysed in terms of the effects it produces outside the country hosting it.

The problem is all the more urgent and difficult to handle with regard to the use and depredation of resources. All natural resources, even those on the verge of exhaustion, are nationally owned. Each nation, moreover, is entitled to harness or waste them according to its interests. Since it confines its analysis to national horizons, Economics is still not equipped to measure correctly the exhaustibility of resources, much less to recommend measures for dealing with the problem. OPEC's decision to raise the price of oil, though positive in terms of conservation on an international scale, was a thumping commercial and financial disaster from the point of view of each importing country. And it was from this angle that Economics analysed it. If the economy (which operates within the legal framework and the prevailing reality of national frontiers) is not to blame, this situation is still proof of the theoretical fragility and internal contradiction of Economics.

The science of Economics remains shackled to a national outlook in an almost entirely internationalized world, not only where relations between people are concerned but also with regard to the effects of each form of production.

For anti-depredatory effects to be taken into account, the sum total of reserves would have to be considered, and protection of reserves would have to have positive repercussions not only for the countries producing the resource but also for those that, as consumers, will be penalized by real scarcity in the future. This will demand great advances not only in the realm of Economics itself but also in the political relations and collective consciousness of the world's population. The science of Economics has been capable of forging an economic reality that is more complex than the models it has managed to frame, given the political limitations imposed upon it. The effects of the economy are international while its measurement is national. Ignoring this political circumstance is to dissociate theoretical models from the real world. Being tethered to present circumstances is to perpetuate models that are incapable of meeting the needs of the day.

The time scale

Another paradox that underscores the backwardness and conceptual frailty of Economics in its dealings with environmental problems (and therefore with modern conundrums) has to do with the treatment of time. Latter-day Economics has begun to take decisions that involve shatteringly large impacts and long-term effects. Despite this, contemporary economists behave in exactly the same way with regard to time as their predecessors, the founders of classicism or neo-classicism, to whom only the short term mattered. Or else, like Marx, they are concerned with the long term only in terms of society's historical tendencies, ignoring real impacts which lie outside their academic hypothesis. On account of the pace at which the process of transforming nature is advancing and the dynamics this imposes on the environment and society, modern capitalism needs to make allowance for both the short term and the long term. Periods spanning a decade can no longer be viewed as being as stable as they were at the beginning of the century or even in the 1950s. Economics will be incapable of incorporating the long term into its analyses so long as its guiding principles are founded upon the maximization of individual interests. Likewise, it will prove incapable of predicting the social and technological changes that will play a decisive part in its analyses.

Measuring the essence

Besides restricting its analysis to the short term and confining it within the bounds of national territories, the science of Economics ignores its ultimate purpose. This may be the result of epistemological alienation, of over-simplification or of some congenital defect. It assumes that the economic process of production is an end in itself. In some cases it actually includes a preoccupation with the distribution of output. But that is as far as it will go. It implicitly associates production with well-being (not to say happiness, which economists steadfastly exclude from their technical terminology) instead of taking production, distribution and the entire economic process as a means of attaining well-being, which includes much more than consumption.

Limiting economic measurement to Gross Domestic Product and its side-kicks tautologically reduces the purpose of Economics to the results of the economy itself. Besides not measuring economic output properly, this indicator is incapable of incorporating the purpose of the economic endeavour to build an intelligent, beautiful, ethical civilization.

Pent up in the prison of the purpose it helped to legitimize, Economics has reached the point of attributing a positive value to the pregnancy of a cow, because it raises GDP, and ascribing a negative one to a woman's pregnancy since it not only hampers her productivity but also diminishes *per capita* income by delivering another human mouth to feed. Society at large, hypnotized by the economic paradigm, has willingly adopted this blinkered approach.

All too often, Economics subsides into economic tautology and stumbles on paradoxes. In its drive to boost output, it disdains the greater values of civilization, such as the pursuit of culture. The urge to raise consumption may have been justifiable in the past when there was a conviction that everyone would some day attain high levels of consumption. However, the more the limits to growth become clear, the more it becomes apparent that the level of consumption is not distributed in an ethically satisfactory manner. When the collective consciousness of a segment of society begins to reject consumerism as the theological *raison d'être* of the civilizational process, there is a pressing need for indicators that measure well-being, indicators not harnessed to, though not necessarily ignoring, the level of consumption. The science of Economics, however, tethered to a tautological concept, refuses to advance towards the adoption of new indicators because it cannot figure out how to quantify them. It does, however, realize that the quantification of GDP, besides being illusory, is imperfect even with regard to the purposes it aims to fulfil.

The prison-house of paradigms

Impact on the environment derives from two vectors that unite to form the ideological bedrock of consumer society. The first is the optimistic view of history and of the infinite capacity for technological innovation which would allow for limitless dynamism in the transformation of nature into goods and services. The second vector is the consumer urge that capitalism has managed to instil into our consciousness. This urge can be identified in the frantic, schizophrenic quest that has become the *causa causans* of economic activity and the objective of the civilizational process.

It is due to the ideology of limitless growth (of which these two vectors are the backbone) that macroeconomics virtually ignores the existence of depredation of resorces and pollution.

It is virtually impossible efficiently to incorporate the environmental equation into economic analysis, given a paradigm in which a drop in consumption is viewed as a setback. Any measure designed for environmental protection has negative effects on consumption. Ascribing a value to nature, levying taxes on pollution, insisting on investment in depolluting filters, additional measures for protection against the risk of nuclear leakages, reforestation, or any other measure that implies additional production costs and sacrifice in terms of the present generation's consumption, thus imposes a choice between consumption or environmental protection. Economics has still not managed to incorporate this choice as a justifiable one, for it still measures performance in terms of increases in consumption.

The challenge of a new formulation

The difficulties of incorporating nature into economic analysis should cause no dismay among economists, especially among young economists about to enter the profession in Third World countries. They must not be taken in by illusions of growth, and they must shun the disguise of modernity. We are experiencing a moment such as Adam Smith experienced when he lived through the transition from a feudal society and mercantile system to the new paradigm of the capitalism that was beginning to take shape, and which he was perceptive enough to detect.

It may take many decades to formulate new principles, to cease observing present deficiencies and studying present proposals for lines of action in order to embark on a real systematization of a new scientific paradigm. This will not be done to counter Economics. Quite the opposite – it will be impossible to accomplish without the science of Economics and will certainly come about with its advancement. But, whatever this advancement may be, it must incorporate nature, as an intrinsic value, into the inventory of the heritage of the human race.

Notes

1. The present author's book *Avaliação Econômica de Projetos* <Economic Assessment of Projects>, Rio de Janeiro, Ed. Campus, 1984, presents a bibliography with 117 titles on this issue.

2. See Ramón Tamames, *Ecología y Desarrollo: La polémica sobre los límites al crecimiento* <Ecology and development: the polemic regarding limits to growth>, Madrid, Alianza Universidad, 1977, p. 78.

3. Ignacy Sachs has written extensive pioneering studies proposing alternative forms of development. On this specific issue, two of his books are essential reading: *Stratégies de l'Écodeveloppement*, Paris, Éditions Ouvrières, 1980, and *Main Trends in Economics*, London, Allen & Unwin, 1970.

4. Two of Josué de Castro's books are essential for assessing his pioneering work: *Geografia da Fome* <The geography of hunger>, São Paulo, Ed. Brasiliense, 1968 (1st ed. 1952), and *Geopolítica da Fome* <The geopolitics of hunger>, Rio de Janeiro, Ed. Cruzeiro, 1947.

5. D. & D. Meadows, *The Limits to Growth*, New York, Universe Books, 1972, and *Toward Global Equilibrium: Collected Papers*, Cambridge, Mass., Wright-Allen Press, 1973.

6. Aurelio Peccei, *Cem Páginas para o Futuro* <A hundred pages to the future>, Brasília, Ed. UnB, 1981.

7. E.F. Schumacher, *Small is Beautiful: Economics as if People Mattered*, New York, Perennial Library/Harper & Row, 1973.

8. Allan Watts, *Le Bouddhisme Zen*, Paris, Petite Bibliothèque Payot.

9. Theodore Rozzak, *The Making of a Counter Culture*, London, Faber & Faber, 1970.

10. Fritjof Capra, *The Tao of Physics*, New York, Bantam Books, 1975; and *The Turning Point*, New York, Bantam Books, 1982; Herman Daly and John B. Cobb,

Economics, Ecology, Ethics: Essays toward Steady-state Economy, San Francisco, W.H. Freeman & Co., 1980; and *For The Common Good*, Boston, Beacon Press, 1989.

11. It is sad to observe, but none the less serves as a lesson for those bent on analysing the political dynamics of the world on the basis of their own desires, how the adoption of a position (even an anti-colonial one) can all too easily become another sort of domination when the struggle to overthrow colonialism is not combined with an internal offensive against local elites. Instead of liberating the peoples of the Middle East, the new oil prices merely fed frenzied binges and spending sprees among their élites. This enabled hundreds of companies from rich countries to get in on the deal and provided international banks with a glut of ready cash which was one of the root causes of the debt crisis that today enslaves poor countries across the globe. The same thing happened to the nationalization of oil production in Brazil, where the 'Our Oil' slogan was and still is used to keep companies committed to a model entirely divorced from Brazilians' real interests.

12. See also W. Leontief, *The Future of World Economy*, Oxford, OUP, 1977.

13. C. Buarque, 'Necessidades Básicas, Avaliação de Projetos e Distribuição de Rendas (entre classes e entre gerações)' <Basic needs, assessment of projects and income distribution (among classes and among generations)>, Text for Discussion, Brasília, Universidade de Brasília, 1979. See particularly Chapter III 'Neomalthusianismo e Avaliação de Projetos: Crítica às Metodologias de avaliação do efeito distributivo dos projetos' <Neo-Malthusianism and project assessment: criticism of methods for assessing the distributive effect of projects>. *Economic prices* here mean market prices corrected to incorporate impacts outside the flow of financial funds from the point of view of business.

14. See C. Buarque, *op. cit.* in n. 1 above.

15. C. Buarque, *Avaliação de Projetos Multinacionais* <Assessment of multinational projects>, a study commissioned by the United Nations Industrial Development Organization (UNIDO) and published as a Text for Discussion by the Economics Department at University of Brasília, 1980.

CHAPTER 8

The Value of Culture

Fear of beauty

Every aesthetic creation is made possible by some prior economic activity. A work of art can only be produced with the use of previously manufactured instruments. Similarly, the free time for its creation must be made available by the production process. Primitive people's creative, aesthetic urge only surfaced when their hunger had been appeased and they were provided with some sort of instrument. Each work of art is thus in itself a product of the economy.

Likewise, the sum total of economic activities should be treated as an elaborate and handsome work of art. Lamentably, economists have never viewed the object of their study as an act of aesthetic creation.

By and large, economists are unconcerned about the aesthetic side of the harmonious order they should be striving to create. They fail to sense the poetry that underlies the transformation of a tree into a pencil that writes a poem, or the mystery of minerals becoming a rocket that goes hurtling into outer space. They cannot appreciate the beauty of the natural world being transformed into goods and services. Much less do they realize that the pencil and the rocket cannot be ends in themselves. They feel no need to explain themselves if their action does not bring harmony among people and between people and nature. They are unconcerned at holding the view that the product justifies itself whether or not it fulfils a higher purpose in the aesthetics of economic output.

In their endeavour to achieve scientific aloofness, economists try to maintain a neutral stance impervious to aesthetic judgements. They yearn to emulate the attitude that physical scientists acquired from the Renaissance onwards once they realized that the laws governing the workings of the universe were not dictated by myths but in fact possessed a life of their own which it was the scientist's task to unveil by neutral observation. Most economists forget that, at the outset, these scientists were impelled by essentially aesthetic concerns in their quest to discern the harmony that lay behind the apparent chaos in the motion of the heavenly bodies. Some economists hunted for mathematical harmony but remained blind to the reality behind their models.

Shortly after he formulated his three laws of celestial movement, Kepler wrote that he might have 'to wait a century for a reader, just as God had waited six thousand years for someone to understand Him'. He saw himself as an observer of a work of art. He was less concerned to discover the logic at work in nature than to ascertain the laws of harmony that it obeyed.

Economists are still basically concerned about the logic of the system they examine, showing little interest in the harmony that should pervade the process of production. They do not even acknowledge that they are part of the movement they study, as one of the decision-making elements capable of influencing its path. They ignore the fact that Economics is capable not only of revealing the logic and the laws of a given harmony but also of formulating the norms for a desired harmony and drafting laws for guiding it.

All that is required is that ethical norms be incorporated into the object of study as the foundations for aesthetic values. For astronomers, beauty is to be sought in the heavens, for economists it should lie in the ethical values they assume.

This has not been done, however. Examining the process of production with a dubious neutrality and taking putatively immutable presuppositions as the point of departure for their analyses, economists have erected an edifice in which the aesthetic value of the economic process is replaced by the quantification of output obtained thereby. Statistics substitute for the beauty of its resonance in the building of a harmonious society.

Economists have shunned sentiment as an instrument for seeking the beauty that should be clearly visible in an efficient process. They ignore the beauty of the way the product is attuned to social harmony. Instead, they have unconsciously assumed that production possesses an intrinsic beauty, regardless of its use, for example of the way that it is attuned to a harmonious society. They have thus legitimized an aesthetics of deformity.

The aesthetics of value

For four thousand years, civilizations have been applying their productive energy to the construction of civil monuments that are devoid of value in terms of material use. The giant Egyptian, Mayan and Aztec pyramids, Christian cathedrals, the monumental stone figures on Easter Island or the triumphant works of the Italian Renaissance were all products of a magic motivation fired by an aesthetic or religious impulse. This motivation could not have materialized if the people who built them had not solved the basic problems of survival. Besides the need to feed the workers, it is difficult to imagine thousands abandoning the fields during harvest or vacating the battlefield in time of war to devote life and limb to the building of monuments. These great constructions could only have been built in times of peace and between harvests. They were, in fact, economically instrumental in mobilizing contingents of idle labourers or slaves and handling 'unemployment'. In a pragmatic though fairly unconscious way, they combined the fulfilment of each individual's spiritual side (through aesthetics and religiosity) with a level of economic efficiency that freed people from the struggle to survive.

The modern world has hampered such pragmatism. It has swelled the contingent of people dispensed from the production of goods for survival, but the magical, aesthetic or religious motivation is sadly lacking. The proportion of workers required for agricultural production has been reduced, but we have generated unemployment in urban areas. We have created a materialistic world in which neither art nor religion is capable of motivating human labour. The problem of the idle masses has grown, allied to the fact that as the market is an instrument of regulation, unemployment represents a loss of economic dynamism. This begets further unemployment, more idleness and the consequent disruption of the social system.

The end of theocracies of the Egyptian, Aztec and Mayan stamp and of medieval Catholicism, growing awareness among modern masses, and the consumer-geared materialism that capitalism creates – these together have all but prevented the building of pyramids and cathedrals amidst a housing crisis.

Even so, future archaeologists may some day come across huge constructions with no real utilitarian purpose as he excavates the ruins of our present civilization. If they manage to surmise the housing standards of the urban population crammed into shanty-towns in big cities of the Third World, they will be hard put to it to explain sophisticated urban infrastructure projects and prestigious government administration buildings.

They might evolve a theory based on an aesthetic-religious motivation in the guise of a cult of value, regardless of the use to which things are put. Belief would then be switched to economic development and the fetishes that its indicators inspire. In this newfangled religion, economists would be cast in the role of modern clergy. Future archaeologists would find, to their surprise, that the ruins unearthed by their excavations were those of a society whose economic activity expressed its mysticism.

An observer uncommitted to the prevailing ideology would have difficulty explaining the paradox of how those wielding the power to transform nature became enslaved by the means they should and could have controlled. Instead of furthering the quest for freedom, science and technology have mostly been used as instruments for boosting output. Freedom is thus confounded with the consumption of material goods which should merely be the foundation for the abolition of necessity. Instead of furnishing more free time, science and technology have kept our noses to the grindstone and foisted upon us the hardships of unemployment. They have even led to forms of alienation in recreation that, rather than fostering greater freedom, often become mechanisms for monopolizing free time. As Sergio C. Buarque puts it: 'compulsory idleness and compulsive labour' have been instated.[1]

Keynes made this point by saying that what mattered was not the value things possessed on account of the use to which they were put but rather the value attributed to them so as to persuade people to work to acquire them. It made no difference if the building of a pyramid were justified on religious grounds or performed in exchange for a wage, so long as the labourer agreed to build it. The national grounds for waging war were irrelevant, provided that young, unemployed warriors could be persuaded to fight, whether in exchange for mercenaries' pay (to be spent on consumer goods for them and their families), or for patriotic reasons. The real justification for war would be the maintenance of industrial dynamics. As he neither believed in religion's power of motivation nor desired the perverse effects of war, to make his metaphorical point Keynes proposed that gold should be buried and people set to prospect for it. At the end of the day, they would queue up to exchange the gold they had dug up for money, and the government would then pay another shift of workers to bury it once more. This vicious circle is no different from the government maintaining an atmosphere of imminent war in order to justify employing people to manufacture armaments. It is also no different from the government purchasing gold that prospectors have panned or unearthed in nature in order to bury it in the Treasury's vaults.

Whatever the hypothesis employed, the Keynesian economic model can only be made operational through a mystical belief in the value of commodities and merchandise. It breaks down the logic of an essential economic process that defines our relation to nature as an instrument of our quest for liberation. The cycle of gold being buried, dug up and buried again makes no sense, like much of the modern production system, even before one considers the social injustice inflicted when output is unevenly distributed. Development should not be criticized – as most economists believe – merely because of the way production is distributed but because of the nature of production itself. Accepting, for the purpose of improving distribution, that production continues to be an instrument for generating employment, economists propose a phantasmagoric model in the guise of scientific knowledge.

Because they fail to entertain the unpredictable facet of the economic process, because they fear to use feeling and ethics as a means of apprehending reality, economists invent a linguistic code to represent the world. This paradoxically lands them in the magical world they seek to escape. But they lack the sentiment required and are short of critical awareness. They confuse the signifier with the signified that the science of Economics has created. Instead of using their aesthetic sense to discern the magical element in economic reality – the incomprehensible, the inexplicable, the illogical – and to take an ethical stand in a bid to check its perverse, ugly effects, economists acquiesce to living in a world where real and intelligible phenomena are jumbled up with imaginary ones, hatched by thought. They are surrounded by their fetishes, and they believe in them. Instead of adopting an aesthetic approach to observing, feeling and interpreting the picture displayed before them, they paint a picture of their own and believe that the figure sketched out has its own life and beauty.

Indicators for gauging economic performance clearly demonstrate this distortion. GDP is the indicator of the total, aggregate value in the economy. There is no inquiry as to what its components really mean and no analysis of the consequences of measuring them. Celso Furtado points up one shortcoming of GDP by stating that a giant traffic jam that delays thousands of people on their way home from work and prevents an ambulance from arriving at a hospital in time is recorded positively in the national accounting because it raises oil consumption – even though that implies the unproductive destruction of irreplaceable fossil fuels. The objective of economic essence has been subverted. People being stranded in a traffic jam will end up in the assets column in the ledger of national annual account-taking.

Such economic indicators are the offspring of a fetish that disguises reality, substituting for it the fictitious world of economic performance statistics. It comes over as essentially positive, even when it produces the opposite of what is desired from the point of view of reason.

Even unambiguously positive indicators, such as employment, are subverted since the purpose of employment is not considered. Military conscription for the mobilization of large contingents of workers for unproductive labour or even for destructive activities is deemed to be a positive feature of the social and economic process. The broadening of our horizon of freedom and the development of our ontological reason are neglected and subverted, making us abject tools for generating value.

To the economist's mind, the aesthetics of transformation becomes an aesthetics of value in itself, of growth divorced from use and cost. Economic laws then proceed to ascribe the same value to coffee produced for drinking and coffee consigned for burning by a government purchasing agency. The side-effects of a giant traffic jam are as valuable as an increase in agricultural yield. An earthquake raises the value of cement-manufacturing industries' stocks, stokes the economy and is thus recorded as a positive occurrence by the economic performance indicator. There is no distinction between a tank and an ambulance, except that the former will have greater weight in economic accounting.

GDP and its quantified growth fail to express the essence of what is desired from and expected of the economy because, by itself, it does not represent harmony in the society that produces it.

To extend its freedom, society needs to break free of necessity and boost the supply of goods at its disposal while reducing the time taken to produce them. But output must be seen as only a part of this process. When it begins to operate independently, it may have the opposite effect. And when economists lose touch with harmony and fail to appreciate the necessary aesthetics of the production process, they fail to grasp the real dimensions and the specific role of economic output in the greater design of human civilization.

In some cases, economic product may sow discord, especially in developing countries. From the second half of this century onwards, they experienced an urge to achieve swift industrial growth, which seriously upset their social harmony. The drive to boost GDP, not as a means but as the central goal of the social process, has become a major source of discord instead of serving to enhance existing harmony. By succeeding in redoubling agricultural production in recent decades, Brazil has managed, ironically, to intensify hunger among its people. In its anxiety to secure industrialization, it has forsaken education. Income was concentrated in order to raise demand through perverse social architecture, and much of the environment was destroyed to boot.

This has not been the fault of a malfunction in the economic model. It is rather the progeny of an efficient economic logic, wholly uncommitted to attaining harmony.

The value of aesthetics

Brazil is renowned for producing some of the best plastic surgeons in the world, especially in the field of rejuvenation surgery, and for displaying one of the highest infant mortality rates. While 87 in every 1,000 newborns die before reaching the age of five, an almost equivalent proportion of upper-class women appear never to age. While the world's finest orthodontists straighten out the slightest imperfection in upper-class children's rows of pearly teeth, two in every three adults have less than half their teeth. While the majority of the population is deprived of access to doctors, a small élite has access to the most sophisticated types of treatment and can resort to a host of world-class psychoanalysts who, in Brazil, probably outnumber their counterparts in European countries. In most cities up to 70% of the population are slum-dwellers while 2-5% bask in luxury mansions designed by some of the world's finest architects.

This distortion, of course, cannot be blamed on those following these professions. Professional vocations are dictated by the market and by a given society's attitude to its problems. In a racially segregated society like South Africa, or in socially segregated societies like those of the Third World, élites who have access to the services of the liberal professions are impervious to the problems of the masses. Even if they did notice them, they would not reckon them to be an attractive market. The glut of orthodontists, psychoanalysts and plastic surgeons contrasts starkly with the dearth of specialists in tropical diseases and sanitary engineers.

The aesthetics which ascribes beauty to value, regardless of its effective results, leads one to attribute value to the aesthetics of professional activities. Instead of serving as instruments for instilling harmony among people and between people and nature (aimed at broadening the horizon of freedom), they dovetail with a global drive to promote economic efficiency that fosters discord.

One of the best examples can be culled from modern architecture in the Third World, especially in Brazil. The dynamic surge of capitalism in these countries, allied to the concentration of income and the creation of a local market, produced a sophisticated breed of architecture of world-class aesthetic standard. Alongside this development, with the exception of isolated attempts made by a handful of researchers, the teaching and practice of architecture have contributed precious little to the search for technical solutions to the severe housing problem which has worsened with the passing of the years. Indeed, modern architecture in Brazil would not have developed so brilliantly had it not been for the low wages paid to construction workers, which have allowed for the most sophisticated experiments in civil engineering. It would not have developed so well had the building materials and financial resources been chanelled into a serious programme for tackling the housing problem. Instead, they were poured into the outsize modern habitations and bulging pockets of the rich and made to aggrandize the machinery of the state. This would not have been possible without whip-cracking governmental authoritarianism which could pool sufficient resources for investing in ambitious engineering projects without needing to justify the expenditure to those who ultimately footed the bill.

Nor did architects have to worry about environmental considerations. Economists furnished the money and the theoretical justification for the use of modern techniques instead of seeking other ways and means of achieving them.

As in Economics, other professions are beginning to acquire an aesthetic purpose that defines their beauty in isolation, alienating them from their potentially liberating roles. They thus relinquish any concern for the social use to which their technical solutions are put. Disdaining the essential purpose of his or her work, each professional unwittingly becomes an agent of economic dynamics by generating employment and creating effective demand for high income. Even artists, whose task it is to build freedom through aesthetic pleasure, abandon the aesthetic value of their works of art (voluntarily or against their will) and proceed to perform the ritual of finding an aesthetics for explaining the economic value their work fetches on the market. Operating like a stock exchange, the arts market then becomes part of the art of the market at the busy hands of the culture industry.

The economist, in turn, is the instrument for making feasible and legitimizing the role of professionals as creators of exchange value instead of value for use. At the same time, economists find in their alienated work proof that their proposals and measures generate a demand which can be gleaned from the Pharaonic buildings, from the flashy health clinics that cater to a sophisticated minority, from the spiralling prices on the arts market. There is thick connivance here, forging a perversely logical pattern with deformed aesthetics, however pure the lines of the artistic brushstrokes it manages to paint may be.

The deformity of production aesthetics, hatching the social monster of Third World industrial societies, finds in economists its great aesthetes and zealous high priests. They legitimize the ritual of hundreds of other professions that have strayed from their essential purposes to partake in the liturgy of economic development, in the accomplishment of an aesthetics of value – often as bloody and inconsequential as the anthropophagic cults of certain primitive religions.

The epistemological gap

Seeking to emulate the work of other scientists, economists have lost track of the quest for creating harmony in society that great physicists have always felt in their investigation of nature.

Unlike the movement of celestial bodies, the structure of the atom or the physiology of the human body, the economic process has unfolded much faster than our imagination's capacity for perceiving it. The physical world (including living organisms) has retained the same structure and the same way of operating since people first attempted to come to terms with it. Physical sciences, like Biology and Medicine, evolve systematically while the objects of their study remain unchanged. The human race has thus had at least 2,500 years of systematic testing of its explanations for the physical world.

Meanwhile, social organization has constantly evolved. Changes in its structure and operation have taken place faster than the social sciences have been able to proffer new explanations. While Physics has been creating increasingly refined models that are closer to the reality Greek atomists examined, the gap between Aristotelian explanations and the Greek economic reality of the 4th century BC was certainly smaller than the chasm that now separates the models mounted by today's principal economists from the complex reality of the world economy. It is an acceptable hypothesis that, despite their sophistication, today's theoretical models reflect less of present reality than the metaphysical lucubrations of the great philosopher reflected the economic reality of his time. Where the capacity for explaining the world that surrounds it is concerned, today's economic science is marked by a great epistemological gap in comparison with Aristotle's science and the object of his study.

The degree of complexity of the real world has grown increasingly distant from the models economists develop to explain it.

The attempt to make Economics follow the same epistemological path as has been trodden by the physical sciences – flatly ignoring the obvious difference in the dynamics of the social process and that of the physical world – is the main cause of the inability of economists to perceive the limits of their science.

The other root cause is the way Economics is taught in universities and research centres. The vice of utter certainty, the conceited belief in consolidated knowledge, the perception of rationality as a constantly improving way forward (provided that neutrality is retained in the relation between the observer and the object of his or her study) prevent universities from developing the aesthetic and ethical side of Economics students. Lacking this vision, they have acquired an uncritical view of their ability to apprehend reality. All too often, the teaching of Economics has been devoted to destroying the slight traces of creative freedom that may have survived secondary school. Lapping up premises considered to be neutral from an ethical point of view, Economics students are enveigled into losing their faith in objectives, replacing it by faith in explanations.

The quest to describe the harmony of reality, so dear to Kepler, has become a search for internal harmony in the model being elaborated, almost regardless of the match between such a model and the reality the economist is striving scientifically to explain.

Technocrat economists prefer to shrug off any commitment to social harmony, worrying exclusively about the balance of the economic system, whatever its consequences for man and society. Economic theoreticians may perceive the tragic side of reality but prefer to alienate their thinking and models, creating idealist abstractions. Both types of economist, either by omission or by connivance, are cast as accomplices in the transformation of the most global of humanity's objects of art – the production process – into the spectacle of deformed aesthetics that modern societies parade before us. This is particularly true in countries where tardy development has been induced by the surgical instruments of Economics, where social concerns have had to bow down to the imperative of economic growth. It is likewise true in countries where cultural values have been trampled under foot by the insatiable urge to consume. It also applies in countries under the iron rule of socialism, where respect for political freedom and freedom of speech have been curtailed by the edicts of economic growth projects, even though such governments justify their actions as a bid to promote justice through the even-handed distribution of income and response to social needs.

Reinventing order

By imposing economic output as the fundamental aesthetic manifestation of the process of civilization, economists have stripped the concept of order of its aesthetic value, which derives from the beauty inherent in the harmony of the social process. They have replaced it with a sense of organization which is a *sine qua non* for the efficient running of the economy. The harmonious order that was supposed to ensue from the conquest of progress has become a pre-condition for conquering progress. Legitimate reasons have thus been found for subjecting social organization to economic purposes.

Explicit or discreet fascism in its various guises – including that by which means of communication and publicity encroach on individual freedom – was to become a framework for social organization, so facilitating the work of economists. In the Third World this was to be the rule in almost all countries governed by authoritarian régimes whose declared intention it was to impose the necessary order for attaining progress.

In socialist countries the organization of production was virtually the same, though they differed substantially in terms of distribution of economic output. In many cases, order in these countries was even more forcefully imposed as the high road to economic progress through social engineering. A rigid social order was set up in order to abolish the role of individual interests and quirks in the operation of the economy.

There have been two main approaches to the issue of order in Economics. The first is that adopted by Adam Smith and all his classical and neo-classical heirs, according to which economic order is merely a manifestation of the natural order of things. People by their unconstrained action, selfishly endeavouring to improve their own personal well-being and fortune, make the economy regulate the existing order – an order of inequalities that can be explained by a wealth of social and psychological models. The second approach to order is that adopted by Marx and, to a greater extent, his followers. To counter the chaos of the natural order of capitalism, they put forward a socially-constructed order, shaped by human will.

The capitalist order has achieved immediate economic efficiency in most production units. Its drawbacks have been inequality resulting from the manipulation of productive forces for the purpose of short-term individual enrichment. It runs a constant risk of chaos and unworkability. Socialism has produced economic inefficiency through unsatisfactory operation of the production system. It has also made for unjustly equal rewards for different amounts of endeavour and degrees of commitment.

What we perceive nowadays, around the world, is an awareness of the fragility of both these approaches to economic order. The individualist capitalist order led to the chaos of people who view each other as enemies and reckon nature to be a foe. People will fight each other and will so callously destroy nature that their own destruction will ensue. In socialist régimes, the social order has bred the chaotic order of the state against the people and of all against nature.

We must therefore strive to re-establish an harmonic order. What is required is an order founded on mechanisms for defending ethical harmony among people and between people and nature. For this to come about, society must be able to rely on economists – provided, that is, that they can overcome their fear of beauty. They must realize the aesthetic role of the harmony of the process by which people manufacture products that serve other people. Finally, they must shape a rationale that incorporates the need for aesthetic purposes into economic value, instead of continuing to assume that economic product has an intrinsic aesthetic value regardless of the social and ethical deformities it has produced.

The value of culture

When one comes across a people whose cuisine is highly inventive it is practically certain that they inhabit a poor environment which bred scarcity and hunger in the past.[2] The result can be fearfully complicated dishes in which the culinary art appears to be cocking a snook at the lack of agricultural resources. The complexity of a people's cuisine is a way of overcoming the historical limitations of economies with a dearth of nutritious products, as is the case in China. The same applies to Afro-Brazilian cookery, which was born of the need of slaves to turn their white masters' left-overs into food of some culinary value. With no access to more nutritious, tasty foodstuffs, they had to pep (and pepper) up their dishes, invent ingredients, and with artistry make them palatable.

Conversely, societies in fertile lands of plenty tend to keep their cuisine plain. This is the case in the *pampas* in South America and the North American Mid-West, where an abundance of meat and cereals has created a naturally rich, nourishing cuisine that requires no sophistication in the kitchen. With plentiful meat and salt, they have no need to go to the lengths of complicated Chinese, Indian or Northeastern Brazilian cookery.

Through its culinary culture, built up over the centuries, society responds to economic difficulties; creativity compensates for the shortage of foodstuffs for placating hunger. With a good dose of imagination, societies manage to transform apparently worthless, unappetizing products into tasty, nutritious dishes.

The culinary phenomenon is a small but extremely representative facet of the relation of culture to the totality of the economic process. Culture is thus an integral part of the economic process, fulfilling its two basic requirements: survival and the achievement of pleasure.

Despite all its refinement, economic theory is no more than a glorified form of cookery in which Gross Domestic Product is a giant cake served up to society. The economic model and technology are the recipe and etiquette determining what is to be considered production, how it is to be implemented given the available resources, who is to be invited to sit at the table, who is to be relegated to the scullery, and what portion of the cake is to fall to each one.

The composition of the product, designed to meet the needs of local consumption, as in a menu, should cater to the tastes and modes of production that best suit the particular culture. However, the culinary art may in many cases in the Third World be the last trace of technology connected with each country's local culture. Even in countries that have imported alternative technology for producing food and obtain a satisfactory supply of agricultural produce, culture fosters an attachment to culinary traditions, resisting new flavours. But as these new options on the menu involve the simplification of production, preserving the necessary nutritious value, the old dishes will tend to be put on the back burner or kept on ice as curiosities or exotic delicacies. This will be a gradual process of cultural acquiescence in which habits and tastes resist and then adjust to the simplification of production just as they previously employed inventiveness to cope with adversity. In this sense, there is a logic in the process. Inventiveness overcomes the dearth of resources, creating cultural habits. Habits, in turn, build up a resistance to the adoption of new, simpler methods and means, which are more efficient in that they require less labour to obtain the product that satisfies needs. But there is constant tension between the production process employed to satisfy needs and the pleasure cultural habits provide.

In recent decades, the production process in the Third World has not respected the value of culture. Economic models and technology have been imported wholesale and instantaneously from developed countries. Underpinning this is a series of assumptions whose acceptance is already two hundred years old. The first is that culture should not be an autonomous input in the production process. On the contrary, it is an output of it. Another is that people from all continents should have a single consumption project and a single technological model.

Some economists have held that a people's cultural traits galvanize or retard the economic system, but that the economic system has its own dynamics that fails to respect these traits. The economy harnesses and applauds culture when it plays a dynamic role and seeks to repress it when it acts as a brake. Marx and Weber attributed an important role to Protestant Reformation in the dynamics of capitalism. Medieval Catholicism and Islam for centuries acted as a restraint on the advance of capitalism. Their dogma condemned to sin those who speculated, did not offer a 'fair price', loaned for profit, or even worked hard out of greed. The Protestant Reformation modified this state of affairs. With its encouragement of honest labour and indignant rejection of the wastage of the nobles and the Catholic church, it played a fundamental part in the culture that was to propel the development of productive forces and the growth of the capitalist economy.

This observation possesses an irrefutable logic, despite the fact that there are two ways of understanding the dynamics of the process: on the one hand, the idealist view that Protestantism responded to a religious need that had economic consequences; on the other, the materialist notion that Protestantism was basically induced by the material forces of capitalism straining to break out of its shell. What unites all streams of economic thinking, however, is a general acceptance that the Reformation was a cultural advance; and that capitalism and the Reformation, by forcibly modifying and modernizing Catholicism, had a positive effect.

Both attitudes disparage the value of the prevailing religious culture in itself. Culture is seen as a consequence and a means of the production process, not as one of its objectives, or even as an input meriting respect for its value.

The Reformation, meanwhile, and all the social upheaval it provoked, were the result of a slow, endogenous process in European societies. By way of contrast, cultural upheaval in the Third World has been instantaneous, induced through the importation of technology aimed at generating the growth of economic forces in these countries.

Third World élites have been hob-nobbing with the populations of rich countries since the days of empire. This has made them a cultural appendix of the metropolis. Besides the influence these élites have exerted on the collective consciousness of their countries, from the beginning of the century a cultural mutation started to take shape among the masses as they began to piece together a dream of development. By the 1950s, a generalized developmentalist conscience had already sprouted and flourished.

Instead of a harmonious cultural evolution, a confusing mixture of cultures resulted. The end of the predominance of rural life came about without the emergence of cities capable of absorbing the flux of migrants; attractive new products were launched but the masses were not rich enough to buy them; new technologies were implemented but the dynamics of the marketplace were not vigorous enough to sustain the level of employment. All this in a period fraught with profound social discord. Keeping things in due perspective, developmentalism over the last few decades has brought results that can be compared with the crushing of the Aztec and Inca cultures.

Unlike the cultural changes that have been taking place in Europe for centuries within the unitary framework of Christianity, in the Third World the process has been imported from abroad and implemented in one fell swoop. Nonchalantly despoiling local culture, it has imposed new values.

From the 1950s onwards, the sudden influx of international capital (no longer in the form of imports and exports but rather in the shape of manufacturing industries) led to the attempt to reproduce in these countries European societies imbued with the selfsame objectives and methods.

Instead of supplying goods to meet the population's needs, using methods suited to the local conditions, environment and culture, this process invented newfangled needs, mustering a competent élite capable of reproducing the manufacturing methods and readily adhering to imported patterns of living and consumption.

The science of Economics was worried neither about being attuned to local culture, nor about the discord it sowed. As opposed to adjusting the economy to local culture, economists declared this culture to be a hindrance to progress and one of the causes of underdevelopment. A long list of works hold that as autochthonous culture is incompatible with development, it is thus primitive, meaning negative. No attempt was made to address culture as an autonomous factor worthy of respect as an input and premise for production. No analysis sought to discover whether the hitch might not be located in the élite's newly imported culture and the wastage of resources that it occasioned, or whether the use of resources poorly adjusted to ecological circumstances was not a flagrant instance of cultural maladjustment.

The upshot was that traditional cultural values were destroyed, with nothing adequate to take their place. The population forgot the solutions it had once known to its problems before learning to respond to imported ones. Its resources were then channelled into implementing unfamiliar projects. People began to be afflicted by desires that their means could not match, such as the purchase of goods costing more than their average monthly income.

As occurs with Third World emigrants who travel to rich countries as unqualified labourers, the people have lost their culture. They have forgotten their mother-tongue before learning the new linguistic code and acquiring new values and tastes. The majority of the population in each developing country has, in a way, been compelled to experience emigration and exile without ever setting foot on foreign soil. For at least a generation, these populations suffer cultural degradation. Individualism, which is the instrument by which people respect one another in rich countries like the United States, becomes an invitation to corruption and violence in newly-developed countries. The lavish consumption that is the hallmark of the final stage of development in almost any society has been the harbinger of concentration of wealth and social segregation in poor countries. Society as a whole has acquired a predatory mode of behaviour before attaining sufficient output to meet its basic needs. People have begun to feel ashamed of their own values, which they now deem primitive and underdeveloped.

In order to build up a humanist economy, economic analysis will have to incorporate each people's culture as both an input with intrinsic value and an end to be pursued. As an input, culture must not only be respected but also used as a lever for galvanizing the economic process instead of being discarded or denounced as a stumbling-block. The Economics applied in each country must make allowance for what its people define as their objectives and how their culture establishes the criteria for organization.

This does not imply chauvinist behaviour, a refusal to participate in cultural activities and employ means already available abroad. It does, however, imply a sovereign approach to defining the objectives society has set itself. Mimicry should be replaced by autonomous definition of objectives (the means for accomplishing them being provided) or else by copying and adapting means already available but for the purpose of serving sovereignly defined objectives.

Among these objectives, the prime one – which embraces the entire outlook of the economic process – is the definition of the sort of progress society desires to achieve.

Notes

1. Sergio C. Buarque, *Ocio Compulsório e Trabalho Compulsivo: Progresso Técnico, Gestão Social do Tempo no Capitalismo Maduro e nas Economias de Industrialização Tardia* <Compulsory idleness and compulsive labour: technical progress, the social administration of time in mature capitalism and in economies that have undergone late industrialization>, mimeographed Masters dissertation, Recife, Federal University of Pernambuco (UFPE), 1985.

2. The first time I came into contact with the idea of a direct relation between cultural, culinary wealth and natural poverty was on reading an article by journalist Gerardo de Melo Mourão in the São Paulo daily, *Folha de São Paulo*.

CHAPTER 9

Thinking in a Third-World World

The century that ended before its time

The 20th century is the first to have begun with a sensation of futurity: by the time it comes to a close, the human race should have inherited a utopian world. From the very first day of 1901, the year 2000 was in the forefront of people's consciousness. The 19th century was depicted as the garden, the 20th as the threshold, but everyone visualized the 21st century as the future: 'There would be world unity, world peace and an ethical system built up without superstitions about death.'[1]

Almost a hundred years on, technology has advanced much further than the dreams of the visionaries. Yet the 20th century has not built the utopia for which people yearned. Indeed, many feel that the world has drifted away from such a state. By carrying out its technological promises before reaching its ordained end, this century has proved that technological accomplishment does not fulfil the dreams of civilization. In a way, the sensation is that the 20th century has ended before its chronological term.

From the point of view of science, the twilight of the 20th century began in 1945 with the euphoria of knowledge and the fear of power instilled by the detonation of the first atom bomb. From another point of view the century dawned and waned at the end of the 1960s when the risks and limitations of economic development were first perceived.

Of all the century's objectives, none has been more dearly desired or more thoroughly accomplished than the dream of a rich, integrated world. Despite this, integration and wealth have brought a bitter feeling of failure. Instead of a global First World, the integrated world has discovered that it is little more than an immense Third World. The earth is an underdeveloped, Third World planet.[2]

Humankind's accomplishment this century has been to make this a poor world divided between poverty and wealth, backwardness and modernity; a planet aware that its social conditions are unsatisfactory because income is concentrated, the environment depredated, and because two-thirds of its population live in obvious misery. This has come about despite the welfare propagated by material wealth.

Yet it is not only economic reality that is unsatisfactory. There is discontent also with the logic that has framed and legitimized this reality over the last few centuries. In the social sciences, particularly Economics, the technical advances that have been a hallmark of this century are no longer sufficient. Alongside the tension between theory and reality, two new tensions arise: between reality and social desires; and between the social object of study (restricted to companies and nations) and a broader scope capable of embracing planetary and ecological dimensions.

The present theoretical framework is too limited to capture our new global reality and the change in desires that are the consequence of this hundred-year process.

From ethics to ethics

Over the last two centuries, Economics has witnessed a procession of interests, schools, crises and models within a single paradigm. Seven premises have laid the foundations of this paradigm: (1) Social evolution is deemed to be leading inexorably to wealth and equity in its distribution. (2) The definition of wealth based on the availability of goods and services; constantly increasing consumption. (3) Value based exclusively on the quantity of labour or people's desires. (4) Scientific neutrality when examining the object of study. (5) The conviction that it is possible to obtain equilibrium in the economic process, along the lines of the way things work with natural movements. (6) The option to limit the object studied to national units. (7) Belief in the advantages of a cosmopolitan world, leading to a uniformity of desires and techniques.

Social scientists' preoccupations have changed, but these premises have remained the same. Comprehension of the economic process and its crises has proceeded without a break in six stages:

(1) From ethics to wealth. From Greek philosophy to scholasticism, thinking has been subordinated to ethical concerns which have been used to explain how production and distribution should operate in order to accomplish the social objectives proposed: cultural enrichment in Aristotle; eternal life among Christians. The mercantilists began to focus debate on the accumulation of wealth, of which gold was the absolute symbol. But it was Adam Smith who lent the problem a thoroughly human dimension. Through him, wealth was defined as the accumulation of material goods manufactured by man, value was linked to human labour, and the workings of the economy were explained according to the natural laws of human egoism and hedonism. By abolishing ethics, Smith unshackled thought and humanized it by placing it within the human domain: our desires and capacity to produce and explain.

(2) From wealth to value. For the first time, wealth was understood as something human beings attributed to things and not as a metaphysical quality, as the scholiasts believed, nor as a quality deriving solely from land, nor even as an exclusive attribute of gold, as the mercantilists reckoned. Adam Smith humanized the problem of humankind by concentrating in men and women the formation and explanation for the value of things. Once the novel idea of economic and material wealth had been accepted, thinking concentrated on studying a scientific problem, through a scientific approach, unhampered by the mysticism of explanatory ethics.

(3) From value to distribution. From Adam Smith onwards, thinkers applied themselves to analysing how value was distributed among people. Maintaining the labour theory of value, many sought to explain how some managed to appropriate value without working. Others repudiated this notion of value and based their explanation of value on the productivity of each separate resource, taking distribution as the natural result of the process in their endeavour to achieve the maximum possible level of output.

(4) From distribution to equilibrium. Partly as an escape from the distributive theme, which ran counter to prevailing interests, and partly in imitation of the conceptions of the natural sciences, economists at the end of the 19th century switched to the study of equilibrium (which can also be traced back to Adam Smith), unconcerned at the constraints of value theory. The 'advantage' of this approach was that it placed Economics on a par with sciences dealing with a world that is not subject to human will and personal values.

(5) From distribution to growth. It was not until the 20th century that the agenda of Economics became dominated by the issue of growth. Ethics, value, distribution and equilibrium are all relegated to a secondary position by the all-important discovery of the mechanisms that promote the growth of wealth. The results proved far better than expected. Since Keynes, output has grown almost uninterruptedly and at high speed. It does now appear to be running out of steam, however.

(6) From growth to ethics. In recent years, in the wake of warnings about limits and risks, the dissatisfaction with growth and the difficulties of establishing equilibrium in economic activity, ethical considerations have begun to creep back into economic discourse. But they are no longer the explanatory ethics or the metaphysics of previous centuries. Smith was humanist to the point of arrogance: he paid no heed to land, culture or time. Newfound wealth was human – neither divine nor metaphysical. Yet it was humanized without being civilized. It was confined to each individual, losing its social dimension. Severing the ties with medievalism, Smith did manage to offer a new concept of wealth, and proved capable of countering the aristocratic view of value derived from land. He failed, however, to perceive the earth as a source of value and the property of all people. Moreover, by stressing materialism he distanced himself from Aristotle. In so doing, he diminished the value of culture.

Adam Smith humanized Economics within the natural constraints of a civilization in possession of limited technical power. By bringing economic thinking down to earth and freeing it from dogma, Smith installed a radical humanism that deified man. He humanized value by reducing the importance of land to no more than a production factor at a time when the human race had not yet acquired the power to destroy the earth on a planetary scale. He humanized the free workings of the economic system at a time when huge conglomerates, the manipulation of statistics and the high-speed transmission of data had not yet attained almost infinite power. He humanized Economics for people with human capabilities, not for people with virtually divine powers. Hedonistic egoism is not the answer in a world in which people can wreak global destruction lasting centuries by wielding technological power in a bid to satisfy their desires.

Homo economicus was thus enthroned as *homo deus*, master of the entire process. He lost his way into the bargain, however, because the economic process had forfeited its higher reason, becoming its own *raison d'être*. The human economy pressed the human race into the service of the economy. People, whose hands gave things worth, began to find worth only in the things their hands moulded, ascribing value according to the time spent making or shaping them. By humanizing themselves to the point of judging themselves to be gods, people made themselves more brutish, bowing down to the things they manufactured. They forfeited a greater purpose for existence (such as culture among the Greeks and heaven among the scholiasts). The process became self-justifying, an end in itself.

If it remains captive to these premises, Economics will not evolve and its intellectual output will fail to make a leap forward both in terms of knowledge and in terms of creating a utopian reality. The earth begins to require a value; nations prove insufficient as accounting units; international trade destroys and concentrates; neutrality ceases to be ethical. By way of reaction, thinking is beginning to change, but it has not yet hit upon a generally accepted paradigm.

From the century of technology to the century of ethics

At the end of the 19th century, Henry Adams wrote: 'At the speed progress has been advancing since 1800, any American alive in the year 2000 will be capable of controlling unlimited force.'[3] He hit the mark in terms of the command of the *knowledge* of force but was wide of it in terms of the ability to control its use. Besides being considered the purpose of civilization, material progress has been confused with technological advance, which has begun to dominate the economic rationale, discarding social objectives and disdaining ethical values.

The reason why Economics is so trussed up in traditional forms of thought is that it has not severed its links with its optimistic view of technology. In recent decades, thinkers the world over have ceased to regard technology as an instrument for subordinating nature to the designs of the human race and now view it as a phenomenon that employs people as an instrument of a project that appears to be autonomous for lack of regulatory ethics. Technologies which were once seen as weapons in the struggle to liberate us from the talons of nature have for decades been demonstrating that they possess autonomous evolution. So much so that society and individuals often adjust their behaviour to them and sacrifice basic interests in order to promote technological progress.[4]

Despite this, established thinking seems aloof from this reality. It continues to abet the production of arms, mechanization (in spite of its perverse features and side-effects) and aspects of medicine that play into the hands of the pharmaceutical and medical equipment industries.

University scientists are still unwilling to view their work as part of a broader project which should therefore be subordinate to social interests. They rally to the call for academic autonomy without noticing the departmentalized prison-cells they inhabit; they defend scientific advance without considering the lack of an ethical or aesthetic purpose; they confound freedom with an absence of ethics.

Given the present circumstances, it is up to universities (more than any other institution) and to Economics (more than any other discipline) to forge an awareness that subordinates technological imperatives to these budding social interests. Technology must no longer be treated as an end in itself but as a means of accomplishing a project of liberation. The order by which technological advance determines the economic rationale that determines social objectives, without the slightest respect for ethical values, must be inverted. Ethical values should be defined first so as to determine the social objectives that will in turn map out an economic rationale that will, only then, narrow the field for selecting the technologies necessary for civilization to advance.

Centuries do not patiently wait for intellectuals to mull over and formulate ideas. If the 20th century has ended before its time without ethics succeeding technology as the key factor in determining social purposes, the 21st century will arrive early, bereft of a clear purpose. Whereas the 20th century bolted from the starting blocks in anticipation of a predictable finish, in possession of a clear-cut paradigm, the 21st century dithers under a pall of uncertainty and doubt.

In the decades ahead, the task of thinking out the future will require navigating on currents of unaccomplished changes, destitute of a paradigm to which to set the compass.

From certainty to doubt

The expectation of certainty arises in the history of thought in the same period as the quest for material wealth in the history of production. Modern Economics and modern epistemology were born at virtually the same time as the Renaissance, cities and mercantilism. Together they constituted modernity in the real world and in the world of ideas.

The world of ideas snatched up the cult of certainty. Ideas shifted from belief to certainty and the hunt for it. This shift was consolidated by the Newtonian revolution which first enabled us to describe the laws of the physical world.

The process was no different in the social sciences. From the advent of the social philosophers, ideas shifted towards explaining social phenomena with an increasing degree of certainty. Although modern thought emerged from the tolerance and scepticism of the 16th century in the minds of Renaissance thinkers such as Erasmus, Rabelais and Montaigne, the following centuries led scepticism to voice a clear preference for certainty as the objective of knowledge. Its spokesmen were Hobbes, Leibnitz and Newton. Belief in medieval, metaphysical dogmatism was succeeded by the equally dogmatic belief in scientific certainty.

The science of Economics was born of this second belief. Like Physics, it sought to explain the movements of the elements involved in the process of transforming nature into goods and services, and in the distribution and consumption of these goods. Like Physics, it believed it could explain the workings of the world with a growing degree of certainty. Adam Smith, Marx, the neo-classicists, modern sociologists and econometricians were propelled by the certainties of their theories.

The world began to change its tune in the 1920s, following the formulation of quantum mechanics concerning indeterminacy in the microscopic universe and under the influence of the laws of uncertainty developed particularly by Heisenberg. Shortly afterwards, the work of anthropologists who undertook the demystification of social evolution, of epistemologists who analysed the unsatisfactory state of knowledge, and the straightforward observation of the relation between theory and reality made the social sciences increasingly uncertain of their theoretical interpretation. This was especially true of Economics, which claims to be the most developed of them all. To crown it all, technologies proved that even technically correct solutions were powerless to deliver the cherished world they set out to build. After swapping medieval beliefs for the epistemological modernization of certainties, with the waning of the Renaissance, the world returned to a period of grappling with uncertainties and doubts.

On gaining the power to probe the intimate recesses of matter, scientists realize that their models describe a world that is already partly a product of observation: it has been transformed by the experiment that attempts to explain it. The social world is even more the result of science and technology themselves, which not only manipulate it but also go so far as to define it, creating a tautology that cancels out its scientific quality.

The speed at which the real world is modified – partly at the hands of science and technology – creates an unavoidable uncertainty among all observers of reality. There is a neck-and-neck race between the formulations that endeavour to explain the object being studied and the transformations this object undergoes, partly as a result of the knowledge social scientists acquire about it. This opens an epistemological gap that may widen rather than close up.

If one compares the pace at which economic reality evolves with the speed of evolution of economic thinking, it is not absurd to raise the hypothesis that Aristotle's crude theoretical devices brought him closer to the true state of the simple economy of his day than the sophisticated dynamic models of a modern economist bring us to our complex contemporary economy. Despite the fact that great theoretical advances from time to time provide a better understanding of reality, the real world of economic activity immediately lurches forward, widening the epistemological gap between theory and reality.

In such circumstances, the notion of certainty, even from the angle of probability, is as idealist an illusion as the idea of the equilibrium of perfect competition. Thinking has become fraught with uncertainties for those desirous to understand the world. The science of Economics will have to admit not only uncertainties but also magic as elements that help us to understand and influence the movements of production and distribution.

Yet the universities are reluctant to cross the threshold into the new age, even though the world is in the throes of another upheaval in the behaviour of knowledge and the methods of apprehending reality. It is still manacled by its faith in the certainties preached in texts set down at the beginning of the century. Rather than gladly accepting the rich epistemological role to be played in questioning through doubt, it lingers in the rut of belief in certitude. It also enslaves most social scientists in the world, goading them into a quest for a certainty that simply does not exist.

'Ecodevelopment' cannot fail to be more than another civilizational project in which science dominates nature and merely seeks to promote a state of equilibrium in the entire ecological system. The crisis that gave rise to ecodevelopment teaches that the arrogant use of science generates imbalances which demand an alternative way of thinking through and understanding the world, not merely one that introduces a different type of transformation. It will have to devise a scientific method in which knowledge 'listens' to nature before selecting the techniques to be employed.[5]

From materialism to a new spirituality

This new epistemology cannot be accommodated in the consumer-based materialism that has underpinned both capitalism and socialism. From the point of view of liberal capitalism, output and consumption are the main goals, religion being conscripted to oil the wheels of social organization without any greater purpose. According to historical materialism, human progress is synonymous with the advancement of the instruments of production.

The general acceptance of this materialist approach reached its zenith in the first half of the 20th century. It now appears to be cooling. After the death of God was decreed in the 1960s, young people, intellectuals and broader sectors of the population began to go in search of new values, looking to the East and to the 'primitive' world for inspiration and renewal.

A number of artists – Picasso and Braque among them – had already taken an interest in primitive art. Philosophers and writers like Huxley, Freud and particularly Jung had dealt with myths – with the permanent values that pre-date capitalist materialism and remain embedded in our recently unearthed collective consciousness. It was in the wake of the turbulent 1960s, however, that this movement expanded with the rediscovery of the East, with the acceptance of alternative modes of thinking, with criticism of rationality and the feasibility of method and, above all, with the acceptance of chaos. The West began to look askance at materialism both as an objective and as a method of thinking. The use of intuition, sentiment and globality was reappraised. The practice of new forms of spirituality, novel for their lack of an inferiority complex, revived. Holism asserted itself as an intellectual praxis.[6]

This praxis, however, has not yet penetrated established thinking, much less the walls of universities, except in a marginal manner at the hands of a few 'alternative' lecturers. Academia scorns studies in alternative fields, which are seen as at best inconsequential. They are treated as a slight to the solid, serious reputation of such institutions and as a depreciation of thought, as opposed to being hailed as a creative contribution to renewal at the present crossroads.

Universities and academia have thus failed to keep abreast of the changes being wrought in the consciousness of a world in transformation.[7]

From specialization to holism

One of the causes of the stodginess that ties universities to traditional modes of thought is their drive to achieve efficiency in specific production through specialization. Specialization allows the world of solid certainties speedily to supply better scientists, technicians and even artists and philosophers. They can more efficiently reproduce and formulate theories for building the utopia of consumption in a satisfactorily materialistic world, albeit in a world in which each intellectual is little more than a node in the vast network for manufacturing material goods and supplying knowledge to raise output. It might even allow itself the luxury of producing occasional cultural goods, provided they are priced and handled as merchandise, tailored to the market.

This approach has proved incapable of producing either the people or the knowledge for a civilizational project which is both efficient and capable of making a better, more beautiful world.[8] In moments of crisis, it does not produce the thinker equipped to formulate a new paradigm for a new age.

A neo-Renaissance figure is required today, and not only in the sphere of thought. The need for such a person is beginning to be felt in technological fields, not just for ethical or aesthetic reasons but also because of the demand for greater efficiency in day-to-day activities. Modern administrative techniques have already noted how fully integrated executives work more efficiently than specialized ones at moments when the future breaks with past trends. Tomorrow's scientists and technologists will have to draw inspiration not only from the theories they have studied but also from the sentiment that derives from the practice of the arts, from the broader understanding afforded by philosophical knowledge and praxis, and from an ethical and political commitment to ensuring that their labour is used in a way that respects other people and the environment. It is becoming apparent that for scientists and technologists to be efficient and competent in their own fields, they will have to be humanized and venture beyond the boundaries of their specializations to gain admittance to a new Renaissance.

The dilemma of specialization and the limitations of Cartesian thinking, as well as the results of technological evolution in itself, have opened up previously unimaginable prospects for fording the Rubicon of this neo-Renaissance and enabling it to flourish. Artificial intelligence, mechanisms for instantaneous global communication, and the general public's exposure to works of art have all given any university student easy access to the work being carried out in other fields. Thanks to the material progress provided by past specialization, modern man can now both act efficiently and experience creative pleasure in his field of specialization. He can likewise practise a wealth of cultural activities in a manner that was open to only very few privileged individuals in the 15th and 16th centuries.[9]

In a way, it is now possible to 'return' to a Greece that no longer requires slaves to sustain the intellectual activities of its philosophers, where the entire population has access to cultural goods and where the masterminds can debate their ideas with all the world on television or through computer link-ups.

This globalization has not yet come about, partly because it runs counter to the interests of a society stuck in the rut of old paradigms, but mostly because universities and intellectuals continue to thwart moves towards it due to an antiquated view of the production of knowledge and a spirit of complacency that shuns change. Our universities thus employ staff poorly prepared to cope with the present or dissatisfied at their current condition. They fail to educate and prepare the competent, fulfilled professionals the future demands and the present already permits.

From theoretical evolution to revolution in thinking

The complacency of the age of certainties in knowledge and of confidence in utopia has led universities at the end of the 20th century to concentrate their competent brains on theoretical advance in each field of knowledge. In the process, however, they have forgotten to contribute to the production of qualitative leaps in thinking. University professors and their pupils, captivated by a global paradigm that appeared to operate efficiently, spared no time for venturing beyond the narrow boundaries of their disciplines. Within their fields, moreover, they scouted no farther than the fences staked out by the theoretical establishment.

Reality demands a different approach. Thinkers, not theorists, are what is needed. Adventures departing from the beaten track, not minor additions to the store of the ageing paradigm, are what is required. As Keynes stated in 1903, referring to his reading, especially of Moore and Russell: 'It was not only overwhelming, but exciting, encouraging, the beginning of a new renaissance, the opening up of a new sky, a new land; we were the precursors of a new revelation; we were afraid of nothing.'[10]

Keynes lived under the illusion of a utopia in which technology was to be the highroad to freedom and cultural production. Thirty years later, he himself was bent on channelling this utopia into production and consumption. With the passage of time, intellectuals have become more and more Keynesian in social and economic terms and less and less Keynesian in intellectual terms: more and more wrapped up in production and consumption; less and less fired by the adventure of a Renaissance. The crisis calls for a reversal: a greater distance from Keynes in economic thinking and greater identity with him in intellectual life.

Universities are not fertile ground for this change, however. The entire academic career-structure and its constraints tend to reward and pamper well-behaved theorists and penalize those who dare cast off the yoke of preordained limitations. Universities are thus destined to bring up the rear in the production of knowledge that will blossom beyond the campus. They will be condemned to the doleful task of picking over, *a posteriori*, the dull theoretical detail of the intrepid thinking daringly unfurled in foreign camps. They seem set to pass up their great opportunity and doomed to fail to fulfil their role.

From traditional anthropocentrism to neo-anthropocentrism

Since the Greeks, modern thinking has been grounded in an arrogant, anthropocentric outlook according to which nature is a foreign phenomenon to be mastered. Material progress from the Industrial Revolution onwards drives this view to extremes of disdain for nature. The human race concentrates all its will-power and endeavours in an attempt to understand nature in order to master it, transforming it into goods and services to be placed at our disposal.

The predicament of recent years compels us to modesty with regard to nature. It is patent that the economic process is jeopardizing fundamental sectors of life on earth, thus threatening the forward march of civilization. We must doff our arrogant disdain for nature and don the modesty of neo-anthropocentrism, showing concern for ecological balance and seeking to converse with the world. We must elaborate a new epistemology in which knowledge is not generated exclusively by a distancing of thought from the object under study, but by a process that places scientists at close quarters and enables them to understand it.

Probably no other phenomenon has gained such ready and widespread general acceptance in universal consciousness as the ubiquitous concern for the environment that we see today. Less than two decades ago this preoccupation was the preserve of a handful of humanists pilloried as mad romantics, reactionaries and sometimes even the agents of imperialism, eager to thwart the endeavours of developing countries to get off the ground. Suddenly the issue is emblazoned on the front covers of magazines across the globe. An assassinated militant rubber-tapper has become a universally acknowledged symbol of the environmental cause. Ecological concern has inspired the biggest ever international political meeting: ECO-92 in Rio de Janeiro.

Universities as institutions, meanwhile, have still not managed to make the leap to embrace this new reality. Economists, sociologists and philosophers have not yet succeeded in turning a preoccupation to a theory. Worse still, they have not incorporated this new-found concern across the academic board.

We are not yet dedicated to grasping the problems involved, to reformulating the theory of value to include nature, in an approach where neo-anthropocentrism will permit us to consider ecological balance as a basic ingredient in the project of human civilization.

From cold war to hot peace

Most of the present generation of university professors were born and brought up under the threat of a global cataclysm: a nuclear war between the two superpowers. Moreover, they viewed the future of the human race through the lens of the bipolar opposition between capitalism and socialism. Only in recent years has a real climate of détente succeeded in dissipating this sense of fear. Other threats have since arisen to take its place. Be they international or local, they have managed to worm their way into the global collective consciousness.

The world whose peace is no longer jeopardized by nuclear conflict now lives in dread of a plethora of baneful phenomena: terrorism, poverty, population explosion, political repression, the tragic blight of localized wars waged with modern conventional weaponry, the searing effects of foreign debt, chaos, the excessive power and inefficiency of states and governments, political and monetary instability, and ecological imbalances. Thinking has also been jarred by the lack of focal points around which to rally.

The world has never experienced such a deep divide as that which now sunders the poor and the rich, creditors and debtors, 'Westerners' and 'fundamentalists'. History – in the sense of contradiction – will only now be free to experiment with all forms of debate. Until now it has been dominated by the socialist-capitalist dilemma under the umbrella of the single paradigm of Western industrial civilization. The difference resided exclusively in how to distribute output. There was no true radicalization to encourage the venturing of all kinds of utopian proposals. For the first time in two hundred years, there are no barriers to prevent the imagination from roaming free through utopia.

From utopia to fear of the future

It was no coincidence that the sense of ideological certainty coincided with absolute faith in the utopia of full supply of goods and services, a faith wrought by science and technology.

From the end of the 1970s, this belief was increasingly called into question. On the one hand, the maturing of existential movements that had been pouring doubt on the values of consumer society reached full bloom in the romantic revolution in which young people in the 1960s engaged. On the other hand, dramatic conclusions about the limits to and risks of economic growth were obtained with the use of long, wide-ranging statistical series, complex systems analyses and powerful data processors.

Drugs, neuroses, violence and boredom express deep-seated dissatisfaction. Pollution, depredation and inequality lay bare the real costs visited upon those prevented from consuming and on future generations. The world then realizes that a utopia founded upon the ontological goals of economic growth and consumption is both unfeasible and unsatisfactory.

Nevertheless, habit has hamstrung the individual consciousness, which still discerns consumption as the central objective of labour. Attachment to the past coupled with perception of its unworkability generate fear rather than paving the way for an alternative project. To cope with novel problems, thinking must break with belief in an obsolete utopia and replace it by new civilizational objectives. Universities plod along in their habitual rut. Their organization, syllabuses and philosophy, their staff and their research continue to wend their lethargic way along the dull cinder path that leads to yesteryear's utopia.

From false equality to social apartheid to real equality

The 20th century has seen the emergence of a belief in the possibility of a world without differences between nations, meaning full equality among people in terms of income and consumption. This belief has been shared by the liberal capitalist economy and the revolutionary socialist state alike.

The end of the century has seen the level of income and consumption of many millions of people rise to First World standards regardless of which country they inhabit. Yet, at the same time, inequalities have worsened and the dream of global identity has not prospered. It is now clear that First World consumption patterns for one and all would rapidly destroy the environment.

Well-off populations are having to pay a high price for the contradiction of a physically integrated but socially divided world: the social degradation of their cities, the risk to the future of their nations, and the ethical demoralization of their societies, compelled to sever their links with the populations of poor countries.

In the Middle Ages, castle walls separated rich from poor. Contemporary social democracies have torn down these ramparts and integrated their poor into society. Sheer distance made it unnecessary to raise walls to keep out the poor from the rest of the world, but the world integration has restored the need for bulwarks and moats to ward off surging migration.

The final moments of the century expose rich countries to a contradiction that has been concealed ever since the Renaissance began defending the idea of equality among people. The idea made Europe ethical and democratic: ethical in the defence of the universal values of freedom and full equality of rights; democratic in the use of each citizen's vote as the means of implementing the values defined by equality.

Two hundred years of economic growth have raised the standard of living of the population of Europe and enhanced the income and consumption of several million people worldwide. The consequence of these benefits has been a radical increase in the gap in consumption levels between them and the majority of the globe's inhabitants whom progress has passed by.

Only at this turn of the century has it become clear that migration of the poor menaces the privileges that the rich have gained and pocketed to date. Wealth gladly displays its condition as a privilege, while the desire for and dream of equality collide with impossibility. The world has marched not to equality but to apartheid, not to identity but to intolerance triggered by difference.

The 20th century, which began with dreams of equality inspired by technical progress and economic growth, now draws to a close with inequalities never witnessed before in the history of the human race. If one considers life expectancy, access to health services and culture, and methods of transport, inequality was less acute between the 17th-century European aristocracy and the masses of peasants than it is today between rich and poor. The aristocracy's doctors possessed resources more similar to those of peasants' in their day than those a middle-class citizen of today's world has in relation to poor people in his country or in the rest of the world. The same applies to means of transportation and food. Even culture – access to which has been considerably expanded for all poor people in the world in relation to the poor of yesterday – presents growing distances owing to advances in the education of the middle and upper classes when compared with the virtual illiteracy of aristocrats before the 19th century. In comparison with the 17th century, almost everyone's lot has improved but the divide has widened.

While the world was physically cleft in two, it was possible to nurture and uphold the idea of equality without actually practising it – much as the Greeks had managed to enshrine the ethics of equality bolstered by slaves, by introducing the artifice of considering them to be essentially different. As the world becomes integrated through communication and transport, the poor draw physically closer to the rich and nurture similar consumption desires, but they lag even farther behind in social terms. Egalitarian discourse becomes fraught with contradiction.

Democracy in each country becomes an instrument for defending privileges against the demands and swelling slum settlements of the poor. International ethics opposes national democracy.

This dilemma is explicitly mirrored in voting preferences in Europe. As democracy is national, it has managed to serve as a stockade against invaders. In Latin American countries where internal inequality makes it impossible to secure the privileges and votes of the poor, there is always the authoritarian spectre lurking around the corner. In South Africa there is racial apartheid and now certainly social apartheid too, since middle-class blacks have acquired the privileges that were previously exclusive to whites. Wherever one turns, the ethics of equality is at odds with the rough-and-ready practice of democracy.

It is no longer a case of direct confrontation between traditional left and right. The defence of privileges and the creation of a world apart will be championed by all those who need to canvass votes among the privileged. The left may well turn out to be an even greater champion of international apartheid because middle-class workers will be more vulnerable than capitalists and the rich.[11]

Inequality is no longer determined by class or country. Nor is it a matter of setting 'rich countries' against 'poor countries', or the proletariat against the bourgeoisie. Countries and classes are as painfully divided as the planet. Rather, it is a matter of confronting those who have been blackballed by progress with those who have reaped its benefits.

Marx's idea of uniting all the workers of the world made sense at a time when the proletariat was reasonably unified and cohesive in Europe, and when there was a clear divide between the proletariat and the bourgeoisie with regard to access to the goods produced. The picture at the end of the 20th century is greatly changed. The proletariat has been riven by its members' integration into or exclusion from modernity, wherever they may reside. Moreover, the lucky ones are no longer so clearly differentiated from other classes in terms of access to consumption. This has wrought an apartheid which divides more on the basis of access to goods and services than on the basis of control of the means of production. The distinction has more to do with consumption standards than with nationality.

In its initial stage, this apartheid drives its wedge through nationalism among the populations of rich countries who nevertheless admit the rich from poor countries into the circle of their acquaintance. The 1950s brought strident nationalism in poor countries struggling to attain the socio-economic standards of rich countries, coupled with internationalization as rich countries sought to expand their economies through the fresh markets of poor countries. In the 1990s the pendulum has swung back, with baleful nationalism brewing in rich countries, anxious to erect barriers to protect the privileges they have amassed. The rich in poor countries, meanwhile, turn to internationalization in order to penetrate affluent markets and keep their incomes on a par with earnings in rich countries. To whatever extent internationalization does actually occur, it will be socially exclusive since it will inevitably fail to incorporate all segments of society. Neo-fascism will not be necessarily or purely racist because it will not debar rich foreigners who boast high levels of consumption, do not compete for scarce jobs, and are integrated into European culture.

The outcome is a trend towards transnational apartheid: an internationalism with those integrated into modernity and all the excluded remainder (including poor youths in rich countries) being separated into opposing camps. In 'rich countries', the majority will vote democratically to preserve privileges keeping the foreign poor at bay. In 'poor countries', the rich minority will find new forms of 'democracy' to keep the majority from impossible mass consumption.

Most intellectuals continue to ignore the dichotomy between global ethics and national democracy. Intellectuals, of course, are not directly menaced by hordes of foreign workers invading their market to compete for their precious jobs and can thus keep up this cool, hypocritical defence of an equality that will never see the light of day. At the same time, they refrain from putting forward alternative proposals for altering the distribution of the benefits of progress on a global scale.

The contradiction between ethics and technocracy will require us to forfeit utopian dreams of equality among people by implementing a rigid system of apartheid which could become genetically consolidated in the coming decades with the aid of biotechnology in fashioning different 'species'. Otherwise, society can settle for differing levels of consumption among people, provided that the basic needs of the entire population are provided for.[12]

Until this century, the production process was basically geared to ensuring survival. A relatively small proportion of output was targeted on luxury consumption. The proportion has since been inverted. Superfluous goods proliferate, gaining ground on those designed for the purposes of survival. This is ample ethical justification for altering the aim of the struggle to bring about equality in consumption.

One of the socialists' mistakes was to believe that after the 1950s equality for all citizens with regard to and for all goods and services was still necessary. As this was physically impossible, they attempted to impose the unworkable equality of expensive luxury items by picking out of a hat those who were to be awarded such products. That made those who had been left out understandably disgruntled, leading them to prefer the market, which left them just as far out in the cold but at least allowed them to feel free of the imposition of the overbearing state and to maintain a spark of hope. The Third World's great error was to nurture the desire to achieve consumption levels to match those of rich countries before guaranteeing basic survival for the masses.

Equality with diversity does not demand access to superfluous goods but it does require that each citizen, the world over, be committed to giving the entire population of the earth the right to basic goods. The integration of the planet into a single system or community must involve extricating the vast majority from their present predicament of absolute poverty. An endeavour must be made to organize the supply and distribution of food products on an international scale, and to provide everyone with access to a minimum of cultural services, such as literacy and basic education, with due respect for cultural diversity. Technologies must also be transferred to all peoples so as to guarantee the entire population of the globe access to public health services, thus eradicating the scourge of endemic diseases.

From national states to diversified cosmopolitanism

The technological advance of recent centuries would have been impossible without the existence of powerful modern states. They made it necessary to pool resources for generating knowledge and guaranteeing a high enough rate of production to foster mass consumption. A number of these states managed to develop such technological prowess and might that their products spanned the globe. But the direct effects of the technologies they employed were confined to their own territories. Despite all kinds of economic, political and military coercion, each nation had the power (in theory, at any rate) to insulate itself from or at least control the effects it imported.

Only recently has the potency of technologies produced effects that reach beyond the frontiers of the countries employing them. Communications make it impossible to insulate oneself from the urge to consume. Nuclear power plants, heavy industry, supertankers, giant dams and reservoirs have introduced ecological modifications on a planetary scale. Technological integration has surprised a world still politically divided.

As Koestler put it, the might of technical reasoning physically integrates a world politically and emotionally divided into tribes.[13] Until recently, there was a general belief that technological integration would lead to political integration by economic means. Recent decades have shown that attachment to the cultural values of each people has been stronger than the economic trend towards integration. At the same time, it is clear that there is no turning back in the process of integration.

The challenge for the coming decades is to manage this irreversible process and at the same time respect the diversity of each person and social group. Moreover, man must strive for the social integration of each individual of the human species in a single, better world where cultural diversity will be acceptable and inequality in consumption patterns will not be at odds with utopian dreams.

European intellectuals do not seem prepared to take up this challenge. In the eyes of European culture, everyone is entitled to be equal, provided that they are not different. Ever since the great discoveries of the 15th and 16th centuries, European humanists like Las Casas have defended the rights of indigenous peoples to become Christians. What they would not countenance, though, was that they continue to be non-Christians.[14] They were just as unwilling to accept the Jews and Moors on the same grounds. Today, religious prejudice against Jews has been dissipated because, culturally speaking, they are as European as the Germans. But animosity towards the Moslems seethes as hot as ever below the surface.

There is no justification for this stance. The world is beginning to realize the importance of cultural diversity, just as the importance of and entitlement to the basic requirements for a decent life have become a matter of consensus.

Universities do not seem to have adapted to this new cultural reality. Even fields of knowledge that should be devoted to coming to grips with the matter – political science and international relations – have done little more than scratch the surface in a manner wholly uncommitted to the modern world.

On the other hand, in an entirely outmoded fashion, many continue to espouse subservient integration of the sort undertaken throughout this century, in which developing countries were viewed as mere appendages of the metropolitan economies. In a hierarchy in which all seemed eager to ape the cultural behaviour of developed nations, local cultures were shrouded in an inferiority complex.

No other group has been as subservient in mimicry of such behavioural patterns as academics. New doctors of philosophy have returned fresh from metropolitan universities imbued with a definite sneering disdain for the local cultures in which they were bred and to which their service should be due.

The distorted viewpoint of undiversified integration stirs up an intrinsic desire across the globe to march towards the kind of development rich countries have promoted. In poor countries, intellectuals create islands of development on which to live, straining every sinew to stamp out the 'old' traits of their societies in an attempt to bring home what they have observed abroad. It is hardly surprising that their societies have become social disaster areas. Eastern Europe, which many looked to for inspiration, is crumbling under the pressure of reality. Despite one of the longest periods of continuous growth in the history of capitalism, developed countries are having to cope with their own set of problems. Tedium, unemployment (albeit remunerated unemployment), wretchedness among limited but growing sectors of their populations, the risk of ecological imbalance, and the ethical degradation to which they resort to defend their privileges – all are turning the resounding triumph of consumer society into a hollow victory.

In spite of this, large sectors of the university commmunity in the Third World still believe in (and ridiculously seek to emulate and revive) the past successes of rich countries. They foolishly fail to grasp the fact that this success is already wearing thin, proving impracticable and undesirable.

In such circumstances, it is up to universities to come to the fore as major agents of the search for and definition of a new modernity, one that will not leave their societies standing in the quagmire, one that learns from the errors committed in Eastern Europe and resists the temptation to imitate developed countries. It must be a modernity that refuses to ape a rapidly ageing form of modernity, one set to advance farther into the future than the staging post of the First World.

From neutral language to ethical language

Never since medieval times have the world's academics and thinkers been as internationally integrated as they are today. In the past, integration extended only to a small group steeped in religious dogma and communicating in Latin on subjects basically related to Theology. They lived in isolation from the population and cut off from the real world. The great scientific discoveries, the Enlightenment and the consolidation of great nation-states broke up this international integration. Such thinking discovered logic, the real world, science and vernacular languages, but reduced global integration.

This century has reinstated integration but in a much more intense, wide-ranging form. Integration has, however, been barred up behind closed doors, defined ideological camps and dogmas, all of them embraced by a single paradigm. The last few decades have witnessed a virtually complete resumption of integration. Yet academic circles remain equally aloof from the population. The prevailing paradigm ensnares thought in the prison of its language.

Since the doctors of Divinity in the Middle Ages, no other group has managed to formulate such a widely-accepted language (or jargon) as 20th-century economists. With the passage of time, words have gone their own way, diverging from the original meaning each one was created to transmit, giving rise to terminological prejudice. It is natural and tolerable that such prejudices should lodge in the collective imagination. It is lamentable that in an institution devoted to thought, such as the university, such prejudices should also have gained legal tender. It is utterly unpardonable that they be deliberately employed to manipulate and disguise reality.

When an economist refers to 'cost', 'balance', 'savage', 'growth', 'demand', 'development' or any other term, he is handling concepts that are unrelated to reality. Each of these terms of economic thought was born at a remove from the reality of the physical and social world. They have been imprisoned in the world of theories and pure concepts, an illusory reality marked out for science. Thought was made the hostage of language and everyone took it at its face value.

Unlike the doctors of Divinity, economists have managed to make their language look legitimate by putting over the idea that the concepts they use are neutral. Now, in a world undergoing upheaval, falsely neutral language is hampering the advance of the science of Economics by assuming it has no ethics when it is, in fact, an ethic that legitimizes one kind of reality through its use.

To free itself from the straitjacket of the present model, science will require a language that recovers ethics – regulatory ethics elaborated to suit the objectives to which society moulds itself. The meanings of this language will have to be related to its purpose: 'demand' approximating to 'need'; 'cost' taking due consideration of ecological destruction; 'savage' meaning all who destroy what logical, ethical, utopian civilization pursues.

This new language of Economics must be first ethical, then systemic and finally mathematical, where possible.

From Economics to Econology

This has been the century of Economics as much as the century of technology. Technology has been the instrument for transforming the world, Economics the rational basis of this transformation. Technology has drawn the current outlines of the world's physical aspect; Economics justifies this outline. To become the century of ethics, the 21st century will have to review the way Economics justifies, explains and intervenes in the world.

It will not be enough for the science of Economics to advance towards reducing the tension between reality and theory. Two new forms of tension that are emerging as we approach the end of the century must be tackled head on. These are tension between reality and social desires; and tension between an object confined to people and their products and a new object capable of incorporating planetary dimensions to the full.

These three forms of tension create three large blocks where thinking must be revised in the years ahead: (1) the scope of the object to be studied; (2) the purposes of social progress; (3) a new rationale capable of serving to fulfil new purposes that take account of a new scope.

The scope

So long as human power was confined to space and time of manageable human dimensions, Economics could be limited to people and their products. The extension of technological power to the planetary scale now demands that the object of study have planetary dimensions; that it include minerals, plants and animals as falling within the scope of the science that studies social movement and transformations.

An ecological Economics should include all the relations of life as part of its study. This means not only incorporating the ecological dimension but also considering the long term. The physical limits of Economics should expand beyond the bounds of companies or nations, encompassing ecology in its entirety. The time span must likewise not be whittled down to the short term, but rather be expanded to take in the future, when the effects of economic decisions will be felt.

It is a case of doing away with the dividing line that separates sciences into those studying minerals, plants and animals, on the one hand, and those that study people and their products, on the other. A logic must be created that will enable us to understand, justify and intervene in the transformation of elements on one side of the divide into those on the other.

The purpose

Increasing material output is no longer a satisfactory or a feasible objective, above all when nature and life are incorporated as part of this objective. Yet the absence of a redefinition of the objectives and destiny one desires for civilization may lead to the temptation to propose a biocentric purpose, in which the balance of nature is in itself the cosmic purpose. In this case, the human race and its products will be seen as part of the universe of minerals, plants and animals. Just as arrogance undermines our civilizational project by setting ecological impact at naught, so biocentrism also disparages it by holding its objectives cheap. By viewing nature as the centre and dethroning the human race, it denies our responsibility.

A new purpose will have to include nature and its balance as an integral part of the objectives of civilization, but it must not stop at that. It must strive to build a civilization on the bedrock of new ethical values in which the purpose will redefine the concept of wealth. No longer restricted solely to material goods, it will include cultural enrichment, ecological balance, the end of basic wants and respect for diversity.

The rationale

Modifications to the scope and purposes of the object of study will demand a rationale different from that which underpins current economic analysis:

(1) Value must be reviewed so as to incorporate nature and collective cultural assets.

(2) The long term must be brought into focus. This implies embracing time and uncertainty as part of the method for monitoring and recording the changing reality of the economy.

(3) National accounting must be redefined. It must include all the new sacrifices and benefits at stake in the natural and human spheres. In

the latter, cultural artefacts and notions that express ethical values, such as justice and solidarity, must be taken on board.

(4) The past evolution of civilization must be reappraised for the purpose of proffering blueprints for an alternative model and denouncing the hazards of building a world containing two separate kinds of people.

(5) The power to regulate must be reconsidered on account of the inconvenience and inefficiency of the forms of social engineering with which the world has already experimented. It must also be understood, however, that the free market is not an effective instrument for raising up a civilization founded on and governed by ethical values.

Technological options must be determined by an economic rationale subordinate to social objectives formulated by ethical values. The hierarchical order: technical values / economic rationale / social objectives / ethical values, would thus be reversed.

The theologians of the modern age

The 20th century has had its theologians. It is economists who have forged a professional language (or jargon) that has gained universal currency. It is they who have pontificated on the sins and virtues of the growth religion. They alone have legitimized and given their blessing to human actions, holding out the paradise of wealth as their reward.

If liberty is a key component of the civilizational venture, one cannot expect any single class, any field of knowledge, or any religious sect to deliver new ethical principles for the world. The new ethics and new proposals will require decades to take shape and set down roots in the collective consciousness, just as progress has taken centuries to assert itself. None the less, new ideas already exist and have been in circulation for years.[15]

The present worldwide repudiation of economists – especially apparent in the Third World – makes it difficult to envisage them being the professional class most intensely involved in the formulation of the new ideas that will circulate until they form an accepted paradigm.

Worse than the rejection to which they are subjected is the conservatism of economists, which makes it virtually impossible for them –

the master builders of the 20th century – to start the ball of proposals for the 21st century rolling. Economists, trussed up in the purposes, rationale and cramped scope of the social object they analyse, can hardly be expected to furnish fresh new thinking. Were they to join forces with other fields of knowledge, however, economists might yet be in a position to shape new thinking that associates Ethics, Ecology and Economics in order to set out the purposes, scope and rationale of a new age. As modern-day theologians, they are the intellectuals most bound to the dogmas they helped to establish. For this very reason, though, they will be in possession of more arguments and endowed with greater legitimacy for criticizing such dogmas and proffering new ideas.

Even economists who perceive and acknowledge the limitations of their knowledge tend to react to new ideas by saying that they fall outside the scope of their science. As they see it, its purpose is to study the way in which the social world produces and distributes goods – without taking the rest of existence into consideration and without furnishing value judgements about the process. They refuse outright to examine our relation to nature and the purpose of civilization for fear that, in searching out the new, they may forfeit old forms of rationality. In broadening the horizons of their thought to encompass other fields, they may lose the bearings of the science they have elected to study. They forget that in moments of crisis no field of knowledge can dredge up solutions from its threadbare, outmoded models. No new way forward can be found unless one is prepared to risk losing one's way, at least the instant before finding the new path to be followed.

Only the taste for intellectual adventure, for daring to chuck out the compass, lose one's reassuring bearings, and have the courage to make mistakes, will allow us to venture into a new field of knowledge; a field in which rationality incorporates new dilemmas and new methods for tackling them; a field where purposes are construed on the basis of new ethical values and where the global scope of the ecological dimension is kept to the forefront of our minds.

Notes

1. Hillel Schwartz, *Century's End*, New York, Bantom Double Bell.

2. A number of social indicators for the World and Brazil are shown in the following table.

	Life ex-pectancy (years)	Calorie/day (% of needs)	Literacy rate (%)	GDP/capita (US$)	Real GDP/capita (US$)	School attendance (years)
World	65.5	113	73	3,140	4,340	5.4
Brazil	65.6	111	79	2,160	4,620	3.3

	1st & 2nd grade enrolments	Scientists/1,000 inhabit.	Univ. students % of same age population	Mortality under fives/1,000 births	Population below the poverty line
World	78	43	3.1	104	29
Brazil	87	30	2.5	85	50

Source: UNDP – Human Development Report – 1991 / UNESCO – World Education Report – 1991.

3. Quoted in Hillel Schwartz, *op. cit.*

4. There is already a long list of authors who, since the 1960s, have been elaborating thought which is critical of technological progress. As early as 1969, Victor C. Ferkiss published a bibliography on this subject containing 320 books in *Technological Man: Myth and Reality*, New York, Mentor Books, 1969. The following, however, deserve special mention: Theodore Roszak, *The Dissenting Academy*, New York, Pantheon, 1968 and his fundamental *The Making of a Counter Culture*, London, Faber & Faber, 1968; Jacques Ellul, *The Technological Society* (trans. John Wilkinson), New York, A.A. Knopf, 1964; Roderick Seidenberg, *Posthistoric Man*, Chapel Hill, N.C., University of North Carolina Press, 1950; John Kenneth Galbraith, *The Affluent Society*, Harmondsworth, Penguin, 1958 and *The New Industrial Society*, Boston, Houghton Mifflin, 1967; Herbert Marcuse, *One-Dimensional Man*, Boston, Beacon Press, 1964; Erich Fromm, *Marx's Concept of Man*, New York, Unger, 1961. For a presentation of the subject, see William Kuhns, *The Post-Industrial Prophets*, New York, Harper & Row, 1971. It was from 1972 onwards, though, that the issue really began to gain momentum, partly due to the publication of the Club of Rome Report, D.H. Meadows, D.L. Meadows, W.W. Behrens III, *The Limits to Growth*, New York, Universe, 1972, and to E.F. Schumacher, *Small is Beautiful*, London, Harper & Row, 1973.

5. Since the beginning of the 1970s, Ignacy Sachs has been fathering the idea of 'ecodevelopment'. See especially his book, *Les Stratégies de l'Ecodéveloppement*, Éditions Ouvrières, 1980.

6. Few books are as important and pioneering in presenting this outlook as Theodore Roszak's *The Making of a Counter Culture*. Chapter VIII, 'Eyes of Flesh, Eyes of Fire', containing an excellent bibliography, is particularly relevant. More recently, no other author has perhaps gone as deep into the subject and done as much to popularize it as Fritjof Capra with his *The Tao of Physics* (1976) and *The Turning Point* (1982). For a yet more recent analysis of the political clout religious movements have mustered in the closing decades of the century, see Gilles Kepel, *La Revanche de Dieu*, Paris, Éditions du Seuil, 1991.

7. Criticism is not levelled exclusively at those searching for new ways of viewing and understanding the world. Russell Jacoby (*The Last Intellectuals: American Culture in the Age of Academy* (1987)) presents a scathing analysis of the bungling incompetence of today's mortarboard bureaucracy that snuffs out any attempt at producing fresh thinking.

8. The alienation rife in intellectual labour, especially among scientists, is depicted in Brian Easley's excellent book *Liberation and the Aims of Science: An Essay on Obstacles to the Building of a Beautiful World*, Brighton, Sussex University Press, 1973.

9. Even the habit and art of letter writing, which the telephone had banished, has been reinstated by the fax, which combines the use of letters with simultaneity of transmission.

10. Quoted by Hillel Schwartz, *op. cit.*

11. It is European workers who are most mobilized and biased against immigrants.

12. In one sense, this is already under way. On a worldwide scale, or within countries like Brazil, available technologies are cultivating stronger, more intelligent strains among the rich, while utter wretchedness is steadily degrading the poor.

13. Arthur Koestler, *Jano: A Summing Up*, London, Hutchinson, 1978. '*Homo sapiens* may be an anomalous biological species, a miscarriage of evolution, affected by an endemic disorder which makes this species different from all other animal species ...'; 'there is a staggering disparity between the growth curves of science and technology, on the one hand, and of ethical conduct, on the other.'

14. On this issue, see Tzvetan Todorov, *La Conquête de l'Amérique: La Question de L'Autre*, Paris, Éditions du Seuil, 1982.

15. The doctoral programme in Ecological Economics coordinated by Manfred Max-Neef now being set up at the Universities of Edinburgh (UK), Gothenburg (Sweden), Concepción (Chile), Brasília (Brazil), and Seville (Spain) is an attempt to lay the foundations of this new form of thinking.

Index

DATE DUE